# Isaiah

F B Hole

**Scripture Truth Publications**

First published as a series entitled "Bible Study — Isaiah" in "Scripture Truth" magazine, Volume 39, 1956-58.

Transferred to Digital Printing 2013

ISBN: 978-0-901860-72-9 (paperback)

A publication of Scripture Truth

Published by Scripture Truth Publications
31-33 Glover Street, Crewe, Cheshire, CW1 3LD

*Scripture Truth is an imprint of Central Bible Hammond Trust, a charitable trust*

We are grateful to Les Hodgett for providing text from a scan of the original articles.
Typesetting by John Rice
Printed and bound by Lightning Source

## PREFACE

Much of the written ministry of Frank Binford Hole (1874-1964) is contained in two periodicals: "Edification" and "Scripture Truth". Between 1956 and 1958 he contributed a series of Bible studies on the book of Isaiah to "Scripture Truth", in which he expounded the prophecy from a dispensational perspective. The richness of references to, and variety of figures used to represent, the great Subject of all Scripture, Christ, is noted from the start. Past and future prophetic applications to Israel are set alongside words of encouragement and challenge for Christians today. References made to the state of Israel at the time of writing have not been updated — the recent history of Israel over the last 50 years only serves to confirm the author's comments.

The publishers of "Scripture Truth" are pleased to bring together these articles in book form for the first time. To assist the twenty-first century reader, minor changes in presentation have been made. The use of quotation (speech) marks has been updated. Scriptural references have been expanded to provide the full title of the book and the format has been standardized to facilitate ease of lookup. All references have been checked, and amended as necessary.

As you trace God's righteousness and grace through Isaiah's prophecy, may a growing appreciation of all God has prepared for Israel on earth and for the Church in heaven, draw out your worship to the One by Whom all this will be achieved.

*John Rice*

July 2013

# CONTENTS

# ISAIAH

## Chapters 1:1 — 4:6

Of all the prophets Isaiah is the richest in the number of his references to the Christ who was to come, and in the variety of the figures under which He is presented to us. It is evident that it divides into three main sections: (1) chapters 1-35, chiefly occupied with pronouncing judgment upon Israel and the nations, but with repeated references to Christ, in whom alone is hope of blessing found. Then (2) chapters 36-39, an historical section, recording God's deliverance, both national and personal, granted to one of the best kings of David's line; recording also how failure marked him. Then lastly (3) chapters 40-66, mainly occupied with predictions concerning the coming Messiah both in His humiliation and in His glory, but presenting it against the dark background of the idolatry of Israel in Isaiah's day, and their rejection of Christ at His first advent.

The break that appears, as we reach chapter 40, is very evident, as also the change in the main themes. So much so that critical and unbelieving theologians have asserted that there must have been several writers or compilers of the book. They speak of two or more Isaiahs. When we turn to New Testament quotations from the book, we find no trace of any such idea. Here is one fact which strongly negatives it.

In the Old Testament God is spoken of as "The Holy One of Israel" only about 37 times. Just 30 of these occur in Isaiah, so it is the characteristic title of God in his book. These 30 are almost equally divided between chapters 1-39 and 40-66, occurring 14 times in the first part and 16 times in the second. This strongly supports unity rather than plurality of authorship.

## CHAPTER 1

The first verse shows that Isaiah's ministry was in the southern kingdom and extended into four reigns. Three of the kings mentioned did mainly what was right, one especially so, and only one — Ahaz — turned aside and did evil. Yet the prophet's opening words reveal a sad state of departure and rebellion among the people. There was not only this, but, as verse 3 states, complete insensibility and indifference. They did not display the instinctive knowledge found in an ox or a donkey. Hence the terrible indictment of verse 4. They were sinful and marked by iniquity, evil-doing, corruption, alienation; and all this was while God-fearing kings were on the throne. It illumines what is said in 2 Chronicles 27, the end of verse 2.

All this had brought upon them the heavy hand of God in discipline and disaster, yet without any reforming effect, as verses 5-9 show. Graphic figures are used to bring home to the people their deplorable state, and verse 9 reveals that only a small remnant existed that God could recognize. Had not that remnant been there, a judgment like to that of Sodom and Gomorrah would have fallen on them. This is ever God's way. Again and again in the past He had maintained a small remnant for Himself in the midst of general departure. He has done so through the church's history. He is doing so today.

Verse 10 has a solemn voice to us. The prophet likens the religious leaders of his day to the rulers and people of those cities of wickedness that centuries before had been destroyed. We say *religious* leaders because of the verses that follow, where they and the people are shown to have been zealous and punctilious observers of the ritual of Judaism. What were they doing? They were offering sacrifices and burnt-offerings, bringing oblations and incense, observing new moons, sabbaths, appointed feasts and assemblies, spreading forth their hands with many prayers. Were not these things right, as ordered through Moses? Yes, they were. Yet all this was declared to be a weariness to God and an abomination in His sight, because, as verses 16 and 17 reveal, their ceremonial exactness was only a decent exterior covering a mass of moral evil and uncleanness. The state of things here exposed blossomed forth into the Pharisaism so trenchantly denounced by our Lord in Matthew 23.

What needed instruction for us! How easy for the present-day Christian to lapse into a similar condition! There are all too many professing Christians who do *forsake* "the assembling of ourselves together" (Hebrews 10:25), for like Demas they love this present age. But what about those of us who *are present*? — even at the prayer-meeting, which many seem to regard as the least interesting of such assemblies. Are we marked by godly and separate living? — by what the apostle James calls, "Pure religion and undefiled" (James 1:27)? — for there is a strong resemblance between his words and verses 16 and 17 of our chapter. Let us never forget that with God right moral condition is far more important than ceremonial exactness in Judaism, or even correct church procedure in

Christianity. If scrupulous ecclesiastical exactitude fosters moral negligence it becomes an abomination to God.

The stern denunciation we have read is followed by a word of grace and forgiveness, a foreshadowing of what we have in the Gospel today. The "all have sinned" of Romans 3 is followed by justification, freely offered through "His grace". Only, the cleansing, offered in verse 18, was in its nature a "passing over" of sins "through the forbearance of God", as stated in Romans 3:25, since the only basis for a cleansing full and eternal lay in the sacrifice of Christ, centuries ahead.

Notice too how "if" occurs in verses 19 and 20. The cleansing and blessing offered hinge upon obedience. To refuse and rebel brings judgment. Both blessing and judgment are concerned with matters of this life, since what is involved in the life to come appears but little in the Old Testament. When the Gospel preacher of today happily and appropriately uses these verses, he of course refers to the eternal consequences of receiving or rejecting the offer, basing what he says on New Testament scripture.

The prophet returns to his denunciation of the existing state of things in verse 21. In verse 24 he announces that the Lord is going to act in judgment, treating them as adversaries; but in the next verse declaring that He will turn His hand upon the remnant, refining them as silver, and purging away their dross. The expression "turn My hand" is also found in Zechariah 13:7, where also, as here, it denotes an action of blessing and not judgment. This is quite plain in the next verses of our chapter. But the redemption of Zion and her converts will be through judgment.

The testimony of Scripture is consistent that the earthly blessing of the coming age will be reached, not by the preaching of the Gospel, but by judgment. This is again declared most plainly when we reach chapter 26:9-10. A clear New Testament corroboration of this is found in Revelation 15:4. This judgment will mean the destruction of the transgressors. They may have forsaken the Lord and turned to false gods with their oaks and gardens, but these evil powers will avail them nothing. All will be consumed together.

## CHAPTER 2

Chapter 1 is introduced as a "vision"; chapter 2 is "the word"; but again concerning Judah and Jerusalem. The opening verses enlarge further upon the good things that will come to pass when redemption by judgment takes place. The first thing is that the house of Jehovah shall be established and exalted. Thus it ever is, and must be. God must have His rightful place, and from that blessing will flow out to men.

But the house of the Lord is here called, very significantly, "the house of the *God of Jacob*", for then God will manifestly have triumphed over the self-centred crookedness that marked Jacob. This will be so clear that all nations will flow to the house to learn of God, so that they may walk in His law. Judgment having been accomplished, men will be marked by obedience Godward, and consequently peace among themselves.

How significant is the word "neither shall they *learn* war any more." Of recent years men have certainly been *learning war*, and all too efficiently have they learned it, so that mortal fear grips their minds. It is beyond the power of mankind to achieve what is predicted in verse 4, though one day they will imagine they have reached it by their own schemes and say, "Peace and safety", only to meet "sudden destruction", as foretold in 1 Thessalonians 5:3.

The succeeding verses of that New Testament chapter are in keeping with verse 5 of our chapter. The house of Jacob is entreated to leave the false lights of their idolatries and walk in "the light of the Lord." That they will do, when the coming age arrives. It is what we are privileged to do today, since we are brought into the light as children of light, and of the day that is to dawn when Christ shall appear.

The prophet returns to the existing state of the people in verses 6-9. From other peoples they had imported various forms of spiritist practices. They were prosperous in material things; plenty of silver and gold and treasures, and also horses, which were a luxury forbidden to Israel's kings, according to Deuteronomy 17:16. All this led to the land being full of idols, before which both poor and great abased themselves. Truly a deplorable state of things.

What then was to be expected? Just that which the prophet now had to announce. He looked beyond the more immediate, disciplinary judgments, that were impending through the Assyrians or Chaldeans, to Jehovah being manifested in His majesty, when His "day" will be introduced. Revelation 6:15-17 gives us an amplification of verses 10, 19 and 21, for men were filled with haughtiness and lofty looks, though they bowed down before their idols.

The list of things, upon which the day of the Lord will fall in judgment, is very impressive. It will evidently make a clean sweep of all the things in which fallen man boasts, even things pleasant and artistic. Instead of accepting and even enlarging the products of man's inventive skill, as an introduction to the millennial age, as some have imagined, it will remove them, as well as the idols and the idolatrous notions that gave them birth. Today men are being humbled as they receive the grace and truth of the Gospel. Then men will be abased and their false glory depart, as the glory of the Lord shines forth.

What then is the spiritual instruction to be derived from this prophetic declaration? The last verse of the chapter supplies it. As it was with Israel in Isaiah's day so in the world today, *man* is catered for, *man* is magnified; but if we "Walk in the light of the Lord" (verse 5), his littleness is seen, and we "cease from man". He is but a dying creature because of his sin. Before God he counts for nothing in himself. We know, in the light of the cross of Christ, that he is worse than nothing. How amazing then is the grace that has stooped to bless such as ourselves.

## CHAPTER 3

Having spoken of the day of the Lord and its effects in chapter 2, Isaiah deals again with the existing state of the people in chapter 3; making plain also how God was chastising them, and would continue to do so. The famine and confusion and oppression, with its accompanying miseries, so that Jerusalem should be ruined, might not come on them immediately, but they would ultimately, though God would favour the righteous as verse 10 indicates. The ancients and princes of the people were the leaders in the evil of that day.

But the evil of the day was not confined to the leaders, or to the men of the nation, such as are described in verses 2 and 3. The women also were deeply implicated. Their state is denounced from verse 16 to the end of the chapter. They adopted all the devices, well practised in the heathen world, in order to increase the seductiveness of their attractions; and, as the closing verses state, the very men they tried to attract should fall by the sword, and so fail them.

## CHAPTER 4

The first verse of chapter 4 completes this grievous theme, and here we believe we do travel on to the last days. The destruction of male life will be so great that women themselves will be found advocating some kind of polygamy to cover the reproach of spinsterhood, prepared to be no real expense to the man whose name they take. This may read strangely to us, but when we consider the predictions of Scripture as to the strife and warfare which will mark the end of the age, we are not surprised. Read, for instance, the prediction as to the warfare "at the time of the end", given in Daniel 11:40-45.

The words "in that day" occur at the beginning of verse 2 as well as in verse 1, and here we see clearly that the "day" in question is the period that introduces the age to come, the time of the second Advent. The word translated "Branch" is used of our Lord five times in the Old Testament, and has the sense of a sprout — "a Sprout of Jehovah for glory and beauty" (New Trans.). Here we see, though somewhat veiled, an allusion to the Deity of the promised Messiah. The figure used is that of a living tree putting forth a sprout which displays its own nature and character. And the living tree here is Jehovah Himself; while the words "for glory and beauty" carry our thoughts to the robes made for Aaron, and to their typical significance as stated in Hebrews 2:7.

Twice in Jeremiah do we get the Lord Jesus alluded to as the Branch, or Sprout (23:5; 33:15); but there what is emphasised is righteousness. It is the character He displays rather than the Source from whence He springs. Again in Zechariah the expression occurs twice (3:8; 6:12). There the emphasis lies on the fact that though He springs forth from Jehovah, He is to take the place of the Servant, and enter into Manhood to serve. Reading the five occurrences in the fuller light of the New Testament, we see how full were these early predictions as to our blessed Lord. The one in our chapter is the first and deepest of them all.

We may remark that Isaiah 11:1 presents the Lord Jesus as a "Rod [or, Shoot — a different word from Sprout] out of the stem of Jesse", and lower down in that chapter He is "a Root of Jesse"; two expressions which remind us of "the Root and the Offspring of David" (Revelation 22:16). "Sprout" of Jehovah is what He was *essentially*. "Shoot" of Jesse and David is what He *became* in His holy Manhood.

Not only will Christ be thus revealed in that day but also a godly remnant will be found, spoken of as "them that are escaped of Israel." This indicates how fierce and destructive of life will be the great tribulation that is elsewhere foretold. Verse 3 enforces the same fact, and from our Lord's prophetic discourse, recorded in three of the Gospels, we learn that Judah and Jerusalem will be the very centre of that time of trial and persecution, which will only be ended when the Lord intervenes in power at His second advent. Those that remain will be alive spiritually and holy, and enjoy the excellent fruits which will be produced by His presence.

But before this happy state of things can be produced there must be that work of cleansing of which verse 4 speaks, described as "a spirit of judgment and by the spirit of burning"; that is, by fire. We may remember that John the Baptist said of our Lord, "He shall baptise you with the Holy Ghost and with fire" (Matthew 3:11). He indicated also that it was the chaff that should be burned, while the wheat was gathered into His garner. In our chapter the wheat is described in verses 2 and 3. The burning of the chaff will purge and wash away the filth.

The cleansing of Jerusalem, indeed of the whole earth, will be by a work of judgment and not by the preaching of grace.

Once judgment has accomplished its cleansing work the presence of God can be restored to Jerusalem, dwelling not merely upon a special building, like the temple in Solomon's day, but rather upon every dwelling-place and convocation. His presence will be signalized as of old by a cloud in the daytime and a flame by night. When that takes place, who shall be able to strike a blow at Jerusalem? The presence of God and the glory accompanying it will be protection. Who can strike through a defence like that?

The word translated "tabernacle" in verse 6 is not the one used for the tabernacle in the wilderness but for the feast of tabernacles or booths. Any extreme, either of heat or of rain, will be so slight that no more than a booth will be needed. Everything necessary will be found in connection with the presence of God in the midst of His people, redeemed by judgment.

The first of the minor sections of the book ends with chapter 4. Consequently we observe that though we have had before us from the outset a very dark picture of the sinful and corrupt state of the people, which would bring upon them the judgment of God, we are conducted at its close to Christ as the Sprout of Jehovah, in whom all hope is found. We shall find this feature repeated. The next section, chapters 5:1 — 9:7, ends with Immanuel. The third section ends, in chapter 12, with the Shoot and Root of Jesse, and the joy that He will bring to pass.

As we further consider Isaiah, we shall note some of those "things concerning Himself" which, when He expounded them on the day of His resurrection to the two disciples going to Emmaus, caused their hearts to burn within them. Considering them rightly, they will have the same effect upon us.

# Chapters 5:1 — 9:7

## CHAPTER 5

Chapter 5 begins with what we may call, The Song of Isaiah. If we turn back to Deuteronomy 32, we may read the song of Moses, which is partly retrospective and partly prophetic. Moses uttered his song at the start of Israel's national history; Isaiah uttered his towards its close. The testimony of both is the same. The failure of the people was complete.

Israel had been Jehovah's vineyard, and He had ordered everything in their favour. A very fruitful spot had been their location with all necessary equipment. The law, given through Moses, had fenced them about, so as to protect them from contamination from outside, if they had observed it. Moreover they were a "choicest vine", for they had descended from Abraham, one of God's choicest saints. Thus everything had been in their favour. What had been the result?

Result there was, but of a wholly worthless and evil sort. Where judgment should have been, oppression was found: where righteousness, only a cry of distress. Once again we have to notice that the charge against them concerns moral depravity rather than lack of ceremonial observances.

When the Lord Jesus spoke of Himself as "the true Vine" (John 15:1), the minds of His disciples may well have turned back to this scripture, as ours also may do. Israel was the picked sample of humanity in which the trial of the whole race took place. The condemnation of Israel is the condemnation of all of us; but it was in the cross of Christ that the condemnation was formally and finally pronounced. The first man and his race condemned and rejected. The Second Man, and those who are of Him and in Him, accepted and established for ever.

The song of Isaiah ended, the prophet dropped figurative language for the hard, plain facts of Israel's sin. Six times over does he utter a "Woe" upon them in verses 8-25, and again we notice that it was their moral evils that stirred the Divine wrath. The first woe is flung at the men of grasping covetousness, who aimed at monopolizing houses and lands for themselves. Judgment in the form of desolation for both houses and lands would fall upon them.

The second woe is against the drunkard and pleasure-seeker. The judgment awaiting them is described down to verse 17. We may observe that similar catastrophe ever follows a people given over to pleasure and debauchery. The great Roman Empire did it in her later years, and then crashed. If Britain and other nations of today do it — what then?

The third woe (verse 18) is uttered against those who sin openly, violently, in defiance of God. The fourth is against men of a subtler type, who overturn all the foundations of right and wrong. Accepting their ideas and teachings the multitude become confused and perverted, condemning what is good and applauding what is evil; truly a terrible state of things.

This leads, no doubt, to what is denounced in the fifth woe. The men who do thus pervert the mental outlook of their fellows, pose as being the wise and prudent leaders of others. At least they consider themselves to be such. And the effect of their teachings — new and progressive, as they would call them — upon those who imbibe them, leads to the denunciation of the sixth woe. They go back to their drink and debauchery, and pervert everything that is right in their dealings with others. If they accept the teaching indicated in verse 20, that is what they will do.

After the second woe no details of what would be involved are given till we reach verse 24. Then the pent-up wrath, merited by the last four woes, is made plain. And in verses 26-30 there is revealed how all six woes would bring upon them chastisement from without. The nations that soon would descend upon them like a roaring lion, and were doubtless headed up in the mighty Assyrian of those days, whom the Lord called "The rod of Mine anger" (chapter 10:5).

## Chapter 6

Having been used to pronounce this six-fold woe, Isaiah was given a vision of the glory of Jehovah on His throne, attended by the angelic seraphim. Of their six wings only two were used for flight. First came the covering of the face in the presence of inscrutable glory; then the covering of their own way from their eyes; lastly their activity in the service of their God; a suitable lesson for ourselves. A spirit of worship and self-forgetfulness precedes service. The very door of the temple was moved at the Divine presence and this was followed by a spiritual movement in Isaiah. It wrought deep conviction of sin and uncleanness, so that having just pronounced in the name of the Lord six woes upon others, he now called for a woe upon himself.

Here we see exemplified the statement, "Verily every man at his best state is altogether vanity" (Psalm 39:5). This happened to Isaiah in the year that King Uzziah died, who was one of the better kings, but ended his days a leper because he dared to push his way into the temple of God. Here Isaiah found himself before God in His temple, and he instinctively used the language of a leper (see Leviticus 13:45), realizing that sin is leprosy of a spiritual sort. No sooner had his confession been made than the way of cleansing was revealed. Live coal that had been in contact with the sacrifice was applied to his lips and the sin and uncleanness removed. Only sacrifice can cleanse sin; a foreshadowing of the death of Christ.

Then came the challenge as to service, and Isaiah's response; and as a result he was specially sent as the messenger to Israel. As often pointed out, the unvarying order is:— first, conviction; second, cleansing; third, commission in the service of God. Isaiah said, "Here am I; *send me*." When God was about to commission Moses, He had the response, in effect, "Here am I; *send somebody else*", as we see in Exodus 4:13; though He overruled it and Moses was sent. Let us all — especially the young Christian — give Isaiah's response and not that of Moses, lest the Lord pass us by, to our loss at the judgment seat of Christ.

It is instructive to note New Testament references to this scene. In John 12:41, the blind rejection of Jesus is the theme, and we discover that Isaiah "saw His glory, and spake of Him." Then in Acts 28:25, Paul refers to our chapter and says, "Well spake the Holy Ghost ...". So here is one of those allusions to the Trinity which are embedded in the Old Testament. In verse 3 we have "Holy", repeated, not twice nor four times, but *three*; and Jehovah of hosts is before us. In verse 5, "the King, the Lord of hosts", whom we find to be the Lord Jesus. In verse 8, "the voice of the Lord," which is claimed as the voice of the Holy Ghost. God is One and yet Three: Three and yet One. Hence, "Whom shall *I* send, and who will go for *US*?"

Verses 9-15 give us the message that Isaiah was commissioned to give. It was indeed of great solemnity. Things had reached such a state that hardening and blindness was to fall on the people, so that conversion and healing would not be theirs, and they would be driven out of their land. The only gleam of hope as to themselves would be found in the fact that God would have His tenth in a holy seed: in other words, He would preserve for Himself a godly remnant. The position was the same among the Jews in Paul's day, as Romans 11 shows, and it is exactly the same today. The national blindness still persists and there is still a believing remnant, but now incorporated in the church.

## CHAPTER 7

With chapter 7 we pass into some historical details of the reign of Ahaz, which are recorded in 2 Kings 15 and 16. He wrought much evil and was now threatened by an alliance against him of Pekah, the usurper on the throne of the ten tribes, and Rezin of Syria. If they had slain or removed Ahaz, they would have broken the line of descent, by which, according to the flesh, Christ came, as indicated in Matthew 1:9. This God was not going to allow, so Isaiah was instructed to take his young son, Shear-Jashub, which means "The remnant shall return", and intercept Ahaz, telling him their scheme should not succeed, and that within 65 years the northern kingdom should be destroyed.

Invited to ask for a sign that should confirm this prophecy, Ahaz declined, not because he had implicit faith in the word of the Lord but because, swayed by his idols, he was indifferent. Nevertheless the great sign was given — Immanuel, born of a virgin — which was indeed valid, both "in the depth" and "in the height above." Notice the order of these two expressions, and then read Ephesians 4:9, where it is emphasized that the descent comes before the ascent on high.

After this prophecy had been fulfilled in the coming of Christ the Jews made great efforts to avoid giving the Hebrew word the force of virgin, treating it as meaning merely a young woman; and to this day unbelievers have followed in their train. The Septuagint version, made by Jews long before the prejudice arose, translated the word by the Greek word which without any question means *virgin*. This one fact effectively destroys the effort to destroy the prophecy.

Verse 15 is admittedly obscure, but we believe it signifies that the coming One, though "GOD with us", is yet, as born of the virgin, to grow up both physically and mentally according to the laws governing human life. This we see to be the case in Luke 2:40-52.

Verse 16 appears to allude to Shear-jashub, who was with Isaiah, for the word translated "child" is not the one so translated in chapter 9:6, but one meaning "lad" or "youth". The prediction of that verse came to pass through the power and rapacity of the Assyrian kings, as the closing verses of this chapter state. The desolations that would follow are then described.

In all this there is only one hope for Israel, or indeed for any of us, and that is, God himself stepping into the scene by way of the virgin birth. Thus was fulfilled the earliest prophecy of all, that "the *Seed* of *the woman*" should be He who would bruise the head of the serpent, the originator of all the sin and sorrow. The virgin birth of Christ is not just a mere detail, an insignificant side issue in the Divine plan. It is fundamental and essential. By it the entail of sin and death, inherent in the race of Adam, was broken. Christ was not "of the earth, earthy", but "the Second Man … the Lord from heaven" (1 Corinthians 15:47). In Him, risen from the dead, a new race of man is begun.

## CHAPTER 8

A second child of Isaiah is mentioned in chapter 8. His long name was significant of the approaching conquest by Assyria of the two powers that were at that moment threatening Judah. Like a flood from the river the king of Assyria would overflow even through Judah, though he was not allowed to take Jerusalem in Hezekiah's time. Assyria did not know then, and the nations have not known since, that the land belongs primarily to Immanuel and only secondarily to the Jew.

Verses 9 and 10 doubtless had an application to the day when Isaiah wrote, but their force abides. Palestine holds a very central position and it is becoming more and more evident that its potential riches are great. The peoples may associate themselves in contending leagues in order to lay hands on it but they will be broken in pieces, "for God is with us"; literally, "for Immanuel". Christ is God; and when He is manifested in His glory, the nations will be as nothing before Him — only "as a drop of a bucket", as presently Isaiah tells us. Among the nations today the idea of a confederacy is strong but this will be the end of it.

Isaiah, however, was warned against the idea of a confederacy for himself and his people. It would be doubly wrong in their case, inasmuch as they had been given the knowledge of God, and He was to be their trust. This we see in verses 11-18. Ahaz in his day was keen on a confederacy, and in the last days there will be strong confederacy between the man, who will become the wilful king and false prophet in Jerusalem, and the predicted head of the revived Roman empire; and this instead of the fear of the Lord.

The reason of this is revealed in verse 15. Immanuel is truly the sanctuary of His people but He would become "a stone of stumbling and for a rock of offence", by the fact of His rejection. This is made quite plain in 1 Peter 2:8. This He is to "both the houses of Israel", though He was rejected mainly at the hands of the house of Judah.

In these striking verses the godly are owned as Immanuel's "disciples". Though the mass of the people fall and are broken, as the Lord said in Matthew 21:44, the testimony and the law will not fail, but will be bound up among those who really fear the Lord. Such will wait upon the Lord instead of turning to confederacies with men, and they will look for the appearing of Immanuel. When He appears in His glory those given to Him, and carried through the time of tribulation, will be for a sign and a wonder. This applies also today, as we see by the quotation in Hebrews 2:13. The saints given to Him today will be manifested with Him in glory. And what a sign and wonder it will be when He thus displays the "exceeding riches of His grace" (Ephesians 2:7).

Verse 19 returns to what was then taking place in Israel. They were turning to the spiritist practices of the heathen with necromancers and soothsayers, trying to get guidance for the living from those who were dead, when the law and testimony was available for them, in which light from God was shining. If they did not speak according to that, there would be "no light in them"; or, "for them there is no daybreak." The principle of all this is more abundantly true for us today, inasmuch as the coming of Christ has so greatly amplified the word and testimony of God, enshrined in the New Testament Scriptures. If men turn from that to the illusive sparks generated by man's wisdom and achievements, there will be no light in them, and no daybreak for them when Christ returns.

Instead of daybreak there will be darkness and gloom, so graphically described in the two verses that close this chapter and the opening verse of chapter 9. There was this darkness in the days of Ahaz. It existed in the day when Christ came, and it will doubtless be very pronounced at the end of the age. The way in which this prophecy is applied to the Lord Jesus and His early ministry, when we turn to Matthew 4:13-16, is very striking. What wonderful spiritual light streamed forth from Him, both in His words and His miracles, for the blessing of those who had been sitting in darkness, whether they had eyes to see it or not.

## CHAPTER 9

The opening verses of chapter 9 follow one another in a very instructive and delightful sequence. Verse 1 continues the picture of *great darkness* and affliction that closed chapter 8. Verse 2 tells of the *great light* that burst in upon the darkness. Verse 3, of the *great joy* that follows; for translation authorities tell us that the word "not" should be deleted. Verse 4 speaks of the *great deliverance* that will be granted: verse 5, of the removal by burning of all that speaks of warfare, so that *great peace* is established.

Referring this to the first advent of the Lord Jesus, as Matthew does, we recognize that these great things have been the result in a spiritual way. They are just what the Gospel brings, whether to Jew or Gentile. They will be achieved for Israel, and indeed for the saved nations, in the coming day when the Lord appears in His glory. Then every oppressor will be completely destroyed and peace will descend upon the earth.

Verse 6 begins with "For"; that is, it supplies the basic reason or ground on which the prophecy rests. The meaning and implications of the great name, Immanuel, are unfolded to us. He is truly the "Child" born to the virgin but He is also the "Son" given. In the fuller light of the New Testament we can see how fitting is the word "given" here rather than "born". He who was "Son" became "seed of David according to the flesh" (Romans 1:3); that is, by His birth of the virgin. Hence His Sonship preceded His birth, and, as the fruit of inspiration, the prophecy was so worded as to be in harmony with the truth later to be revealed.

The government is to rest on the shoulder of Immanuel, and the full import of the name is now given to us under five headings. The first is "Wonderful"; that is, Singular and beyond all powers of human scrutiny. Then He is "Counsellor"; One involved in the counselling which precedes Divine acts, as for instance, "Let Us make man ..." (Genesis 1:26). This must be so inasmuch as He is "Mighty God". Again, being so, when He takes flesh and blood, His name of course must be "God with us". Moreover, He is "Father of eternity", as more literally the words read. Eternity has its origin in Him. The ascription of Deity to the Child born could not be more distinct.

Lastly, being all this, He is "Prince of peace", the only One who, in this rebellious world, can establish it upon a permanent basis. This He will do by the warrior judgments predicted in verses 4 and 5. Becoming "Seed of David", as we have seen, He will sit upon the throne of David, and having crushed man's rebellion and evil, He will govern with judgment and justice to the glory of God and the blessing of men. The Second Advent of our Lord will see these great predictions fulfilled to the letter.

The epoch in which we live is not the day of God's government upon the earth but the day of His grace, when government is still in the hands of the Gentiles and God is gathering out of the nations a people for His name. The time of grace may soon end, and then God will arise to deal with the world problems created by the sin of man. To bring the whole earth into subjection will indeed be a colossal task, but as our scripture says, "The zeal of the Lord of Hosts will perform this." We may well rejoice that so it will be.

# Chapters 9:8 — 14:32

At this point the prophet resumed the denunciation of the people and their sins, which had been suspended that he might relate his vision of Jehovah of Hosts and give the prediction concerning Immanuel. We now learn how God's hand was stretched out upon them in anger and discipline. In chapter 5, woe was pronounced upon them six times, and now we get the hand of God stretched out in wrath four times over — verses 12, 17, 21, and 10:4. There seems to be an increase of severity as we proceed.

The ten tribes had been chastised with much destruction, but in their pride they declared that it gave them the opportunity to rebuild on a much improved scale. They spoke then just as men are speaking today as they view the destruction wrought in the recent war. The Lord warned them that their ally, Rezin of Syria, would be overthrown, a token of the overthrow coming upon themselves.

But again the people did not accept the discipline and turn to God who sent it. Consequently they would be deceived by prophecy that was false, and from the highest to the lowest face a cutting off and disaster. But this too would fail of any true effect.

Hence further miseries would come upon them and inter-tribal strife. The wrath of the Lord would darken the land and yet be as a fire and the people as fuel. And still His anger would remain.

## CHAPTER 10

They would still practice deceit and treachery and oppression, and bring upon themselves what is described as "the day of visitation". Having forsaken their God, He would be no refuge for them in that hour of distress, and His hand would still be against them. This brings us to the Assyrian, in verse 5.

But we pause a moment to remark that, as so often in Old Testament prophecy, there is an ultimate fulfilment as well as a more immediate one, and this surely is the case here. For instance, there were prophets speaking falsely in Isaiah's day, but the very special "prophet that speaketh lies", who is "the tail" {9:15}, is a reference to the antichrist of the last days; just as "the day of visitation" looks on to that special day of trial that is yet to come. Similarly "the Assyrian", that now we are to consider, has this double application — the then existing great power centred in Nineveh, and also that "king of the North", which was Assyria, that we read of in the last days.

In Isaiah's day the power of Assyria was threatening all the nations. God had taken that people up as the rod of His anger to chastise many a nation that was far from Him — and Israel among them. Later God used the Chaldeans in the same way, and this it was that disturbed the mind of Habakkuk, and led him to protest that, bad as Israel might be, the Chaldeans, whom God was going to use against them for their discipline, were worse. We see here what we see also in Habakkuk; that God may use an evil nation to chastise His faithless people, but only under His strict supervision and control. God was now sending him, as verse 6 says, against an hypocritical nation — evidently the ten tribes and Samaria.

But the Assyrian himself did not realize this, and therefore "he meaneth not so", but intended to ravage Jerusalem as well as Samaria, doing to them what he had already done to many of the surrounding peoples. As we know from the historical Scriptures, though he distressed and threatened Jerusalem he did not take it. As verse 12 intimates, he would be used to perform on Jerusalem that which God intended and then he himself would be punished and humbled. He was only like an axe or a rod in the hand of the Lord and could not dictate to the One who wielded him. The Holy One of Israel would consume him and bring down his pride and importance.

We know how all this was fulfilled in the days of Hezekiah. Samaria was led captive, but when Sennacherib attempted with proud boasts to take Jerusalem his forces received a conclusive blow directly from the hand of God, and he himself was shortly after slain by two of his sons, as we read in 2 Kings 19:37.

The double application of the latter part of chapter 10 is, we think, quite evident. In verses 20-23, God pledges Himself to preserve a remnant though He was to permit a great consuming in the land, according to His holy government. This promise of a remnant covers the whole "house of Jacob", for it must have been given some years before the ten tribes were taken into captivity. God did preserve a remnant in those far-off days when the prophecy was given, and He will yet do so in the coming days at the end of this age.

So again, in verses 24-34, there was the plain assurance to the inhabitants of Jerusalem that they need not fear the

Assyrian. He would afflict them as with a rod, yet God would destroy him eventually. This came to pass, as we have seen, though he would come to the very gates of the city and "shake his hand against the mount of the daughter of Zion, the hill of Jerusalem." His progress through the towns, as he approached, is very graphically described. He would seem to be like a great cedar of Lebanon, stretching his mighty bough over the city, but Jehovah of hosts would lop his bough with terror.

## CHAPTER 11

All this also has an application to the last days, as is manifest when we commence reading chapter 11, for there is really no break between the two chapters. The Lord Jesus is the "Rod [or, Shoot] out of the stem of Jesse", and the "Branch", and the chapter presents Him in the power and glory of His second coming. That the Spirit of the Lord, in seven-fold fulness, rested upon Him at His first coming is very true, and when we read of our Lord that "God giveth not the Spirit by measure" (John 3:34), there may be a reference to what is stated here, as also there is in "the seven Spirits" mentioned in Revelation 1:4; 3:1; 4:5; 5:6; and in this last reference they are "sent forth into all the earth", as will be the case when the Shoot of Jesse comes forth endowed with this seven-fold fulness.

We are reminded also of the candlestick in the Tabernacle with its six branches springing from the main stem. The oil, typical of the Holy Spirit, fed its seven lamps. The "Branch" is to grow or, more accurately, "be fruitful", and when Christ in the plenitude of the Spirit fills the earth, fruit will abound for there will not only be wisdom, but the might to enforce its dictates, and all controlled by the fear of the Lord.

Moreover He will not be dependent, as are human judges, on external things; on what He sees or hears; since He will possess that "quick understanding", which will give Him that intuitive knowledge, which springs from His Divine nature, so that His actions, whether in favour of the poor and meek or against the wicked, will be marked by absolute righteousness. At last an age of righteousness will have dawned.

As the result of this, peace will descend upon the earth, so much so that all antagonism and ferocity will depart, even from the animal creation. The creature was made subject to vanity, not of its own will but by reason of the sin of Adam, and it is to be "delivered from the bondage of corruption" (Romans 8:20-21); but the Apostle gives us a detail not made known to Isaiah, for it will be the time when not only the Shoot of Jesse will be manifested, but also the manifestation and glory of the sons of God.

The picture of millennial blessedness, presented to us in verses 6-9, is a very delightful one. Missionaries would tell us, we believe, that to slay and eat a kid of the goats is a special attraction for the leopard, just as the wolf naturally slaughters the lambs. All creation shall be at peace, all ferocity abolished; even the poisonous serpent deprived of its venom and its desire to bite. The earth in that day, instead of being full of the confusion and the conflicts created by the fall of man, will be full of the knowledge of the Lord as the waters cover the sea. How do the waters cover the sea-bed? They do so completely, without one crevice being unfilled. Such is the lovely picture that is presented to us here.

And how can such wonderful things, not only for Israel but for all creation, be brought about? Verse 10, we think, sheds light on this, for there we discover that the Lord

Jesus is predicted as the "Root of Jesse", as well as a "Shoot" out of his stem. We are reminded at once that in the last chapter of the Bible the Lord presents Himself to us as "the root and offspring of David"; an allusion doubtless to our chapter. Here "Jesse" is used, we believe, to heighten the contrast, for David had become a name of great renown, whereas Jesse only reminds us of the otherwise unknown farmer from whom David sprang. From one small and unknown the great Messiah was to spring, and yet to be the Root from which Jesse sprang.

So, if as the Shoot we think of Christ in His holy Manhood, as the Root we have to think of Him in His Deity. In His Manhood He sprang out of Israel, and had special links with that people. Introduce His Godhead, and all men come at once into view. So it is, as often noticed, in the Gospel of John, where the word "world" occurs with great frequency; and so it is here, for the word "people" in our version should be "peoples"; that is, the nations generally, to whom the Root will stand as an "ensign" or "banner", and to Him will the Gentiles seek: and "His rest will be glory", as the margin reads. Greed will go out and glory will come in. What a day for the earth that will be!

This wonderful prophetic strain continues to the end of chapter 12, and four times do we get the expression "in that day". The first we have glanced at in verse 10, when the promised Messiah shall be manifested in His Godhead glory, and bring blessing to the remotest peoples. The second is in verse 11, for in that day there will be a regathering of Israel, and the predictions concerning this continue to the end of the chapter. We must not mistake the present migration of Jews to Palestine for this, since verse 11 speaks of what will be accomplished in the day of Christ's manifestation, and it will be an act of God and doubtless accomplished through Christ; for "Lord" in verse 11 is not "Jehovah" but "Adonai", the title used for instance in Psalm 110:1, when David by the Spirit spoke of the coming Messiah as "my Lord".

Moreover, when that re-gathering is brought to pass, the division between the ten tribes and the two will have disappeared, and the nations that surround Israel will have been subdued, and there will be an alteration in geographical conditions both as to Egypt and Assyria. None of these things have yet come to pass.

But these things will come to pass, and "in that day", when they do, there will burst forth from Israel a song of praise far deeper and more sincere than that which was sung in Exodus 15. But let us recapitulate for a moment. In verse 10, Messiah appears in His Deity and glory as the rallying centre for all mankind. He draws all to Himself, according to John 12:32. But this means, as the rest of the chapter shows, that Israel will get redemption blessing, far more wonderful than their past redemption from Egypt. Then follows, as chapter 12 opens, the triumph song of this new redemption. Jehovah had been angry with them, and rightly so in view of their past of tragic wickedness, but now He has become their Comforter, their Strength and their Salvation.

## CHAPTER 12

If verses 1 and 2 remind us of Exodus 14 and 15, verse 3 is reminiscent of Elim, which is mentioned in the last verse of chapter 15. The Elim wells were very welcome and refreshing but here is something far more wonderful, of which Elim was only a faint type, since the salvation that Israel will then receive will be not only of a temporal sort but also spiritual and eternal.

Our short chapter ends with praise in view of that which will be the very climax of their blessing — the "Holy One of Israel" in the midst of them. This was foreshadowed when, redeemed from Egypt, the Tabernacle was erected in their midst with the cloud of glory resting on it. This which will be brought to pass "in that day" will far exceed what was accomplished under Moses. With this striking prophecy a definite division of the book reaches its close.

## Chapter 13

What we have seen we might almost call, *the burden of Jacob*. Judgment has to "begin at the house of God" (1 Peter 4:17). Israel was that of old time, but though their heavy guilt brings on them heavy judgment, a bright future waits for them at the end. The judgment having begun at them, we now find the surrounding nations judged. A burden lay upon them from the hand of God and as the prophet uttered the burden it lay also doubtless on his own spirit. Chapter 13 begins the "burden of Babylon". The Spirit of God foresaw that this city would become the chief oppressor, and the original seat of Gentile power when the "times of the Gentiles" should set in.

The predicted destruction will arrive when "the day of the Lord" sets in, as verses 6 and 9 show; hence the terrible overthrow, detailed in verses 1-16, will be witnessed in the last days, and be executed upon the proud Gentile power of which Babylon was the head and front, as we see in Daniel 2 and 7. Verse 11 speaks of punishing "*the world*" for their iniquity, and of convulsions in the heavens as well as the earth, such as the Lord also predicted in His prophetic discourse. But in verse 17 the prophecy does descend to a judgment more immediate, which was executed by the Medes, as the book of Daniel records. It is in this connection that the statement is made that the destruction of Babylon should be complete and irremediable. The prediction has been fulfilled unto this day and still stands. Anything that might appear to be to the contrary applies, we judge, to the dominant Gentile power, which does still exist, and of which Babylon was the beginning, or to that "mystery" Babylon of Revelation 17, which represents the false professing church, left for judgment when the Lord comes for His true saints.

## CHAPTER 14

The first three verses of chapter 14 show that the judgment of Babylon clears the way for mercy to flow to Israel. This had a partial fulfilment in the days of Cyrus, as the opening verses of Ezra record. It will have a far greater and more complete one when the times of the Gentiles come to an end. Then, not only will Israel be established once more in their own land but they will be the supreme nation, ruling over the others who formerly oppressed them, and completely at rest themselves. In that day they will take up the proverb against the king of Babylon, that fills verses 4-23 of the chapter.

When Isaiah uttered this prophecy Babylon was still dominated by the Assyrian power. A century or so later it became "the golden city" under the great king Nebuchadnezzar, spoken of as the "head of gold" in Daniel 2:38. With him the times of the Gentiles began, and they will close under the potentate, called "the beast" in Revelation 13, who is to be raised up and inspired by Satan, who is called "the dragon". All the world will worship the beast and the dragon who, though unseen, lies behind him.

Isaiah's prophecy in these verses applies first to the visible king — verses 4-11. The Lord will break his sceptre and cast him into hell as is more fully explained in Revelation

19. But in verses 12-15 we seem to pass from the visible king to Satan, whose nominee he is to be. Satan, whose original sin was an attempt at self-exaltation unto equality with God, is to be "brought down to hell, to the sides of the pit", as we also see in Revelation 20.

Verses 13 and 14 are most striking. Notice the five-fold repetition of "I will". The very essence of sin is the assertion of the will of the creature against the Creator. In Genesis 2, God said to Adam, "Thou shalt not"; but in Genesis 3, tempted by Satan, Adam virtually said, "I will". The complete contrast to this is found in Philippians 2, where the One who *was* "the Most High", whose throne *was* "above the stars of God", who could not "ascend", since there was *no place higher* than the one He occupied, *descended* and took the form of a Servant. Satan sought to exalt himself and is to be abased. Christ humbled Himself, and He is, and shall yet be, exalted.

In the succeeding verses we seem to come back to the judgment of the visible king, of his city, and of all those that follow him. It will be no partial or provisional dealing of God but a final judgment that will make a clean sweep of his power and kingdom, a judgment more severe than that which has fallen upon others.

At verse 24 we pass back again to the more immediate judgment of Assyria. Upon the mountains of Israel, which the Lord calls "My mountains", he should be broken. This had not been accomplished in the year that king Ahaz died, for that was the third year of king Hoshea of the ten tribes, and Samaria was carried captive by the Assyrian in Hoshea's ninth year. In verses 29 and 31 "Palestina" means apparently "Philistia", the country to the south west of Jerusalem. At that moment all might seem peaceful, but their judgment was coming, and their only hope and trust was to be reposing in Zion.

Now Zion does not mean simply Jerusalem, for that city too would ultimately fall under God's judgment. Zion was founded by the Lord in His mercy when He intervened and raised up David, so that it has become a symbol of the mercy and grace of God. This we see in such a scripture as Hebrews 12:22. In that grace, which Zion represents, the godly poor amongst the people will trust. They *did so* in days that are past. They *will do so* in days that are to come.

They *are doing so* today. *Are we amongst them?*

# Chapters 15:1 — 23:18

## CHAPTER 15

It is clear that, when God acts in judgment, He begins at the innermost circle. It was so in the days of Jerusalem, as we see in Ezekiel 9:6, and the same principle holds good in New Testament times, as stated in 1 Peter 4:17. In Isaiah we have seen the predictions of judgment first uttered against Israel, though with promises of restoration and glory in their Messiah. After this follows the judgment of the nations surrounding Israel.

We have seen Babylon head the list, to which judgment is prophetically meted out without any promise of restoration. Now in chapters 15 and 16, Moab comes into view, a people that in its origin stood in a distant relationship with Israel. Against them too judgment is pronounced but with a note of sympathy (see, 15:5) which is altogether absent in the case of Babylon. The Moabites were a pastoral people but dwelling on high ground east of the Dead Sea and strongly fortified. In verse 1, Ar is the city and Kir the fortress. All should be laid waste.

## CHAPTER 16

The prophecy refers to judgment which would speedily fall on Moab in view of their haughty pride, as the last verse of chapter 16 shows. The opening verse of that chapter also refers to the tribute that Moab used to pay, as we see in 2 Kings 3:4. Yet in part the prophecy also refers to the last days, for verse 5 looks on to a King "in the tabernacle of David", whose throne will be established, and who will be "hasting righteousness." Before that hour strikes God will have a people whom He calls His, though they are "outcasts" in the earth, and Moab will do well to give them shelter. That Moab will exist in the last days is made clear in Daniel 11:41, as we saw also in our prophet, when considering chapter 11:14.

## CHAPTER 17

In the days of Isaiah, Damascus had been allied with the ten tribes. Its "burden" fills the three verses that open chapter 17. The prophetic strain however quickly passes from Damascus to the children of Israel for disaster was to come on both, since both had united in alliance against Judah. The figure is used of harvest, whether of corn or of grapes, which would leave them poor and thin, yet a remnant would be left, like a gleaning of grapes or a few berries on an olive tree, and that remnant will turn their eyes to "the Holy One of Israel", and away from the idolatrous things that formerly held them.

All this found a fulfilment in days immediately ahead, yet will have an ampler fulfilment in the last days yet to come. The prediction about the "pleasant plants", or "plantations", and the "strange slips" is often referred to in connection with the recent doings of Jewish immigrants in Palestine. They have indeed been busy with plantations in their agricultural colonies and have imported vast quantities of vine cuttings from other lands in order to re-establish vineyards.

But look at verse 11, which predicts that, though this work will have a promising beginning, it will suffer a crushing blow. And, how? By a great and antagonistic uprising among the nations, of which the rest of the chapter speaks. Here doubtless we have a brief yet comprehensive sight of the final convulsions among the nations, when God will make Jerusalem "a cup of trembling" and a "burdensome stone" to all the peoples round about, and "gather all nations against Jerusalem to battle" (Zechariah 12:2-3; 14:2). Jerusalem and the Jews will indeed be heavily chastised, but the proud nations themselves will meet ultimately the fury of God and be scattered before Him, like chaff or thistle-down is blown away by a whirlwind. As we view present doings in Palestine let us not forget this solemn prediction.

## CHAPTER 18

Chapter 18 opens with a call to a distant land that is to serve God's purpose in the last days, helping to regather Israel. Verses 4-6 appear to be parenthetical, so that verse 7 is connected with verse 3. Both verses 2 and 7 speak of a people "scattered and peeled [or ravaged]", who without a question are those we now know as Jews. Our chapter indicates that, when in the last days God gives the signal for their regathering, there will be a distant people with ships who will do what they can to help them. But the parenthetical verses show that, though God overrules this, He is not directly acting in it. He retires, as it were, saying, "I will take My rest", observing what is taking place, but ultimately bringing disaster upon it all, as we saw in the previous chapter.

And yet, in spite of all this, the scattered and ravaged people will be recovered and brought as a present unto the Lord. Verse 7 does not tell us how this is to be accomplished after the failure of the earlier attempt. When we read Matthew 24:31, we find the Lord shedding light on this matter. The people who will be brought thus as a present to the Lord will be "His elect", and not just an assortment of patriots and fugitives, as we see at present. And they will be brought "to the place of the name of the Lord of Hosts, the mount Zion." Alas! Jerusalem as it is at present cannot be designated thus. It is the place where Jews are reassembling, hoping to display the greatness of their own name, while still rejecting their Messiah.

The Jew has yet to discover the meaning of "the mount Zion"; namely, grace flowing out from God, rather than merit through law-keeping, achieved by themselves. The Apostle Paul realized this, as we see at the end of Romans 11. They have been shut up in unbelief, "that He might have mercy upon all." The contemplation of this over-abounding mercy to Israel moved Paul to the doxology, concerning God's wisdom and ways, with which that chapter closes.

## CHAPTER 19

We resume the "burdens" on the surrounding nations, as we read chapter 19. Egypt, that had so much to do with Israel and its history, now comes before us. Again we notice the feature so common in these prophecies: the predictions soon pass from more immediate judgments to those that will mature at the end of the age. History tells us that soon after Isaiah's day Egypt did fall from her former high estate, and things recounted in verses 1-10 came upon them. The princes of Zoan did become fools, though in the days of Moses long before "the wisdom of Egypt" was highly regarded.

Yet in the latter part of this chapter the terms of the prophecy go beyond anything that has transpired in the past, and so look on to the end of the age. This is corroborated if we turn to the closing part of Daniel 11, where "the king of the south" represents Egypt, and we are told how Egypt will yet be overrun and plundered by "the king of the north" in the last days. In those days "the land of Judah shall be a terror unto Egypt", and this certainly has not taken place yet, though it may do very soon.

Out of all this discipline, which yet is to fall on the land of Egypt, some spiritual good will come. Egypt has been in the past well filled with altars to their false gods and with pillars erected in honour of their despotic kings. It is going to have an altar to the Lord in its midst and a pillar to the Lord on its border. Not *many* of either, you notice, but *one* only, for by then they will acknowledge the one true God. Though He smites them for their sins, He will heal them and send them a deliverer. At the last Egypt will know and do homage to Jehovah.

The three closing verses of this chapter are a remarkable prophecy, for Assyria — the king of the north, of Daniel 11 — was the great oppressor of Israel in the days of their kingdom, just as Egypt was the oppressor in the days of their early servitude. In the last days all the enmity will be banished. An highway with free communication will extend between them, and Israel will be in the centre. Egypt will be blessed as "My people"; Assyria as "the work of My hands"; Israel acknowledged as "My inheritance". To be Jehovah's inheritance is something greater than to be His people or His handiwork, yet all here is connected with God's purpose for earthly blessing. What is stated does not rise to the height of Ephesians 1:18, or Colossians 1:12, yet it does enhance our sense of the mercy of God as we note that finally He will act in blessing to both peoples, who have been in the past, and will yet be, Israel's inveterate enemies.

## CHAPTER **20**

The short chapter 20 brings us back to events that were to happen, shortly after Isaiah was bidden to enforce his prophecy by a peculiar action. He foretold the coming overthrow of Egypt by his walking naked and barefoot. Other prophets, such as Hosea, were instructed to support their words by actions. The object in view was to bring home to the inhabitants of this "isle", or "coast", that is, Palestine, that it was folly to put their trust in Egypt for deliverance from Assyria. It will doubtless be the same in the last days, as we see in Daniel 11:36-45, where "the king" of verse 36, who will evidently be in Jerusalem, will find no help in "the king of the south" against the assault of "the king of the north".

## CHAPTER **21**

In chapter 21 we return to the doom of Babylon. It is to be "the desert of the sea." In Jeremiah's prophecy against the city he says, "The sea is come up upon Babylon" (51:42), which helps to explain the expression. Babylon would be swamped by the sea of nations and become a desert. In verse 2 the call comes to Elam and Media to go up and besiege, helped to the spoil by treachery. Verses 3-5 prophetically describe in the most graphic language the scenes of revelry, turning into confusion and terror, which are described for us in Daniel 5. Then the prophet foresees a watchman, who from an oncoming chariot gets the tidings of the fall of Babylon, and announces it with a voice like the roar of a lion.

The burden of Dumah is compressed into very few words. He was, as Genesis 25:14 shows, of the stock of Ishmael, and Seir was a dwelling-place of the sons of Esau. These "burdens" on the various peoples were bringing upon them a "night" of Divine displeasure. What was the

45

prospect that lay before them? The answer was indeed prophetic. A morning was surely coming, but a night was coming also. The morning will be for those who fear God and are subject to Him: the night for those who are His foes.

In other scriptures very strong judgment is pronounced against Seir, but verse 12 here indicates that a door of mercy will open to them. If any have a desire to enquire of God they may do so. And if, as the result of enquiry, any desire to return, they may do so. They are even invited to "come." In these words we discern an indication and forecast of that grace which comes to light so fully in the New Testament Gospel.

At the close of the chapter Arabia comes under judgment. Disaster should overtake them too, but not in such over-whelming fashion as in the case of Babylon. Their mighty men should be "diminished", and there should be a "residue", and not a complete destruction. It is striking that of all these burdens the one upon Babylon is the most complete without any hope of recovery. So also in Revelation 17 and 18, the "Mystery" Babylon is going to be completely destroyed and not a trace left.

## CHAPTER 22

But Jerusalem too must come under judgment, as we see in chapter 22; and here again, as is so often the case, and particularly when Israel is in view, we find a double fulfil-ment contemplated. The prophet sees the city, once full of joy, now full of misery and sorrow. It was "the valley of vision", but now the vision had perished, and the valley was full of besieging chariots. And in this dire emergency instead of turning to God in repentance and seeking His mercy, they busied themselves in taking all the measures of defence that they knew, and then settled down to enjoy themselves, even if death came on the morrow.

"Let us eat and drink; for tomorrow we shall die" is the reckless cry of men who know there is danger ahead, but are determined to have their fling before it arrives. The Apostle Paul quoted these words in 1 Corinthians 15:32, showing that if this transient life were all, and there were no resurrection of the dead, such a reckless attitude might be justified. We have come to an age in the world's history when men are aware of awful dangers ahead, and with no real faith in the resurrection world, this ancient saying is in control of their lives. With no fear of God before their eyes, millions are determined to get all the pleasure possible out of life with the hope that death ends all. We are to be marked by a spirit which is exactly the opposite of this, and to be always abounding in the work of the Lord, knowing that there is the resurrection world, and that our labour is not in vain in the Lord.

Let us also remember that in an emergency it would be quite natural for us to do in principle what Israel was doing, as the enemy threatened them. They adopted what looked like wise military strategy instead of turning to God, which would have involved weeping, sackcloth and repentance, such as marked Nineveh in Jonah's day. The flesh in us would prefer *policy*, that appears so wise, rather than *penitence*, that costs so much to our pride.

This thought is emphasised by the episode regarding Shebna and Eliakim, recorded at the end of the chapter. Shebna was a man with much riches passing through his hand for he was the treasurer. Thus he had distinction in this life, and building for himself "a sepulchre on high", he desired to perpetuate his memory when his life was over. Self-exaltation was evidently his aim. He was rejected, and

God would dispossess him so effectively that the chariots of his glory would turn out to be the shame of his lord's house, as we see at the end of verse 18.

Shebna then was rejected and Eliakim, whose name appears to mean, "God is setting up", was to take his place. This transfer actually took place during the reign of Hezekiah, according to the word of the prophet, but we see in it a parable of what will take place at the end of the age, when the self-exalting "man of sin" will be violently turned and tossed to destruction, and the once rejected Christ shall be exalted and established. Of Him Eliakim, in this incident, was a faint type.

This is evident when we read Revelation 3:7, and note how our Lord claims for Himself the very things that are said of Eliakim in verse 22 of our chapter. He it is who is worthy to have the government laid upon His shoulder, not only of Jerusalem and Israel but of the whole universe. He it is who will hold the key of David and will unlock and bring to light and establish "the sure mercies of David", of which we read in chapter 55. Eliakim doubt-less had a place of much authority under Hezekiah, but the graphic and conclusive figures, we find here, go far beyond him.

Notice three things. First, the key and the opening or shutting of the door, which no man can reverse. No such door has ever yet been found under the control of mere man. The authority and power indicated is Divine.

Second, "the nail in a sure place". What place on earth is sure? Where has such a nail been found? The nail more-over is to be "for a glorious throne to his father's house", and to have "all the glory of his father's house" hung upon him. Great statements these! They only find proper fulfil-ment in our Lord Jesus Christ, for indeed, not only the glory of the house of David hangs upon Him, but also the glory of God that is found in redemption.

But now, third, there comes the paradox. The nail that is fastened in the sure place is to "be removed, and be cut down and fall". Here surely we have one of those partly hidden references to the rejection and death of the Messiah which the Old Testament furnishes. In the light of the New Testament all becomes clear. He will be manifested as the Master of every situation, and as the One upon whom everything hangs in the coming age, *just because,*

> "By weakness and defeat
> He won the meed and crown."

So in the end of our chapter we have a reference prophetically to the removal of the man of sin and the establishment of God's Man — the Son of Man — in His excellence, maintaining the glory of God and the blessing of men.

## CHAPTER 23

The series of burdens ends in chapter 23 with "The burden of Tyre." In those days this very ancient city was the great centre of trade and commerce. This is quite evident in verse 8 of our chapter. In the days of David and Solomon its kings had been very favourably disposed and helpful, but its great wealth and prosperity had wrought corruption, as seems always to be the case in this fallen world. In this chapter Isaiah predicts a period of disaster and eclipse that should come upon the city, but with some respite at the end of seventy years.

The great Nebuchadnezzar laid siege to Tyre and this is referred to in Ezekiel 29:18, which speaks of his having "no wages" for the long years he spent over it, for the

Tyrians had time to remove all their treasure. Still judgment from God did come on the proud and rich and joyous city, and her glory departed.

The comparative mildness of the burden on Tyre is accounted for, we believe, by the fact that it was not an oppressor of Israel. It presents to us a picture, not of the world as oppressing and enslaving the people of God, but as the scene of man's successful and opulent activities in forgetfulness and independence of God.

Thus, in the chapters we have been considering, we have seen the world in all its aspects, both secular and religious, brought under the judgment of God. Yet in the midst of the judgments are a few bright flashes of light, which direct our thoughts to the One in whom is found the centre of all blessing — CHRIST.

# Chapters 24:1 — 27:13

## CHAPTER 24

The last of these cities, upon which a "burden" rested, being disposed of, the prophetic strain moves on to make known in a more general way what would be the state of things at the end of the age. It is a dark and sorrowful picture: the whole earth turned upside down and the inhabitants scattered, no matter to what class they belonged. And not only Israel is in view, for though the closing accusations of verse 5 may have special reference to them, since laws and ordinances were specially given to them, the covenant of law, given at Sinai, could not be termed "everlasting". The reference here is rather to the covenant established with Noah and the new world of nations of which he was the head, according to Genesis 9:9.

The first 12 verses of the chapter are filled with the gloom of earthly judgments, but when we reach verse 13 light begins to break, for a remnant of God-fearing ones is indicated, under the same figure as was used in chapter 17:6. So that, even in the darkest hour, a note of praise will be sounded and God will be acknowledged and honoured;

and that in all parts, for "the fires" is a poetic expression for the east and "isles of the sea" for the west.

Thus God will have His witnesses in all parts, though in the presence of abounding evil and the judgments of God they may only be conscious of their leanness. Thus indeed it ever is and must be with God's true servants. It is the false who speak of their fatness, as "rich and increased with goods". God may empower His servants by His Spirit, but they are conscious of nothing but leanness in themselves.

Verses 17-20 give us a graphic description of the terrible overturning of all human order and institutions that lies ahead. Six times in these verses is "the earth" mentioned, referring rather to the established order and world-system of things than to the actual earth-crust on which we live. All will be violently shaken before they are removed by the presence of the Lord.

The three verses that close the chapter show the effect of His presence. Not only will punishment fall on the kings of the earth but also "the host of the high ones ... on high" will be judged and "shut up in the prison". What this means comes out more fully in the book of Revelation, where we learn of Satan and his angels being cast out of the heavens, and then Satan himself bound in the abyss, when the kings of the earth, under the leadership of the beast, are consigned to their doom. God will judge not only the nations but also the Satanic powers behind the nations. We get a glimpse of these powers in Daniel 10:13, 20.

Then shall be established a new order of things in the presence of which the very institutions of heaven will be confounded, for Jehovah of hosts will reign in glory "before His ancients". This is a remarkable word. He does not reign *over* His ancients when He reigns in Zion and Jerusalem, but *before* them. They are witnesses of His glory, and remind us of the "elders" of Revelation 5. The word here might be translated "elders", we understand, which confirms the thought.

And, who is this Jehovah of hosts? He is evidently "the King of glory", but, as Psalm 24 asks twice, "Who is this King of glory?" We know He is the One who bowed His sacred head in death for our sakes, according to Psalm 22. So our chapter ends with the power of evil — both in its fountain head and in its ramifications — smitten from the earth and the Lord Jesus enthroned at earth's centre and reigning before the delighted eyes of His ancients.

## Chapter 25

No wonder therefore that chapter 25 opens with a note of praise. The Lord will then have visibly done wonderful things, and His counsels of old will have been fulfilled in faithfulness and truth. When these things come to pass it will be easy to sing the note of praise, but it is our privilege as Christians to praise before they have come to pass: to —

> "Sing — till heaven and earth surprising,
> Reigns the Nazarene alone."

When the glad millennial day dawns it will mean the overthrow of man's strong cities and of the terrible nations that built them. It will also mean the shelter and uplifting of the godly remnant, as indicated in verse 4. Jehovah will prove Himself to be for them "a refuge from the storm, a shadow from the heat". We turn to chapter 32:2 and we find that the same two things are to be found in a Man: truly an extraordinary statement, for an ordinary man in a tornado is but the sport of the elements and no refuge at all. In very deed, the MAN of chapter 32 is no ordinary man, but to be identified with the Jehovah of our chapter. We know Him as the Lord Jesus Christ.

The power of the great adversary, and of the nations who have become his tools, having been disposed of, full earthly blessing will be brought to pass, described as a feast of fat things and of old, well-matured wine. It may have been to this that our Lord referred, when He uttered the words recorded in Matthew 26:29. The day of earthly joy is coming, and it will extend to "all peoples", for the word there is in the plural. Yet the centre of it will be "this mountain", referring to mount Zion, mentioned in the last verse of the previous chapter. Jerusalem doubtless is indicated, but mentioned in such a way as to emphasise that the blessing will be given as an act of *mercy* and not as the reward of *merit*.

Moreover, there will be a work Divinely wrought in the hearts of all who enter that glad age. The power of the adversary has cast a covering, or a vail over all the peoples, and it will be completely removed. The Apostle Paul uses a similar figure in 2 Corinthians 3 and 4, only applying it more particularly to Israel, based upon the vail that Moses wore. Yet he makes it more general in chapter 4, when he claimed that he put no vail on the Gospel he preached, and that any vail that existed had its seat in those that were lost. When today the vail is lifted from a sinner's eyes, and he discovers his Saviour, it is the gracious work of the Spirit of God. Today it is an individual matter. In that day it will be on a world-wide scale, and it will result in the discovery that is brought before us in verse 9.

But we must not overlook the great statements of verse 8, particularly the one that Paul quotes in 1 Corinthians 15:54 as finding fulfilment in the day of resurrection. Whether the saints who lived before Christ came discerned the resurrection in these glorious words may be open to question, but we now know what they infer, and in the faith of them the victory enters our hearts, and we have it before the actual day of resurrection dawns. Death being removed, the tears, that by reason of it have been on innumerable faces, will be wiped away for ever, and the "rebuke", or "reproach", of His people will be gone for ever too. Primarily no doubt, His "people" here refers to the redeemed and born again Israel, who will enter the millennial age.

But it will be true for all saints — those who by resurrection enter the heavenly world, as well as those blessed upon the earth. Through all the ages God's saints have walked in reproach. Enoch must have looked odd in his day, and certainly Abraham in his. From a worldly standpoint how foolish of Moses to leave the splendid place he had in the court of Pharaoh! And so we might continue till we come to Paul and his associates who were "fools for Christ's sake". What are we who profess the name of Christ? Have we so accommodated ourselves to the spirit of the age that reproach for Christ is hardly known by us? If so, we shall miss in large measure the thrill of that hour, which will surely come, for "the Lord hath spoken it."

The salvation which will reach Israel in that day will be wholly and obviously of the Lord, and publicly owned as such. The godly, who will enjoy the salvation, will be those who have ceased from their own efforts and have waited for Him to intervene on their behalf, just as today the sinner who receives the salvation of his soul does so when he learns to condemn himself, ends his strivings, and trusts in the Saviour. Then too he gets deliverance from his spiritual foes, just as Israel will get deliverance from Moab and other enemies, as the closing verses of our chapter show. In that day they will exclaim as they see the glorified Jesus, "Lo, this is our God".

## CHAPTER 26

Then, in the opening verse of chapter 26, we get the jubilant song that will be heard in the land of Judah in that day. The prophecy still centres geographically in Jerusalem and mount Zion. The city will at last be strong inasmuch as its protection will be the salvation which God will have appointed. No other city has been besieged so often as Jerusalem, but at last its sorrows will be over, and its inhabitants be described as "the righteous nation which keepeth the truth".

The sequence of thought here is to be noted. First, salvation; then, righteousness; thirdly, peace. But peace is to be enjoyed as the mind and heart is stayed in simple trust on the Lord. Hence the exhortation of verse 4, where the name of the Almighty is, so to speak, duplicated. It is "JAH-JEHOVAH", to emphasize that He is indeed "the Rock of Ages" — as shown in the margin of our reference bibles. Isaiah uttered this exhortation to the men of his day, before God's delivering might was manifested. It is equally valid for us today; indeed more so, since to us God has been made known in Christ in a far more intimate way.

But this deliverance for the godly will involve the work of judgment upon the world of the ungodly, as verses 5-11 show. God is presented as the most "Upright" One in verse 7. He weighs the path of the just, which has a character in keeping with Himself. So, while the godly wait for His judgments to be made manifest, His name is the object of their desire and they are sustained by the remembrance of Him as He had been revealed to them. This saying is sometimes linked with 1 Corinthians 11:24-25, "in remembrance of Me", and not unjustly, we think. Only, their desires and remembrance will be directed to One who had made Himself known to them in the past by deliverance through judgment. We remember the One who expressed Divine love through death on our behalf, while our desire goes out for His return in glory.

This passage is in complete accord with the fact that the Gospel is being preached not to convert the world but to gather out of it "a people for His name" (Acts 15:14). Favour has been "shewed to the wicked" for over nineteen centuries, and unrighteousness is still as rampant, if not more rampant, than ever. The hour approaches when God's judgments will be let loose in all the earth, and then at last those who come out of the judgments will have learned righteousness. Verse 10 also shows that what is wrong is not merely man's circumstances but man himself. Put "the wicked" into "the land of uprightness" and still "will he deal unjustly". Many an ardent Communist or Socialist agitates, and labours to improve the conditions under which the masses of mankind live, under the mistaken notion that granted right conditions all would be well. The fact is that the root of the evil lies in man, and the wrong conditions have been created by him. Put fallen man in his unconverted state into the most ideal conditions and he will overturn and mar them.

In verses 12-18, the prophet addresses the Lord on behalf of the remnant who fear Him. He confesses what a redeemed Israel will be brought to confess in the coming day. The peace that they then will enjoy is wholly the work of God. They will no longer speak of their works but of the works He had wrought on their behalf. Then as a result of this they are delivered from the old idolatrous powers that formerly lorded it over them. No other name but that of Jehovah will be on their lips, and the very memory of their dead idols will have perished. Then they confess that only under the chastisements that God inflicted on them have they turned to Him and been increased. Their own efforts produced no deliverance for themselves nor for the earth.

Verses 19-21 give the answer of God to this prayer of confession. "Thy dead shall live, My dead bodies shall arise" (New Trans.). Here we have in a brief statement what is given in more detail in Ezekiel 37, and alluded to in Daniel 12:2 — the national reviving of Israel, when God raises up and gathers His elect. They had been dwelling "in dust" — or, as it is put in Daniel, sleeping "in the dust of the earth" — they were to awake and sing. It is worthy of note that, when proving to the Sadducees from Scripture the fact of the resurrection, our Lord did not quote these scriptures but went back to His words to Moses.

Though many Jews are now back in the land of their fathers this national reviving of a spiritual sort has not yet come to pass, nor will it until "the indignation" of verse 20 has taken place. We identify the "indignation" with the "great tribulation" of Matthew 24:21, which in its most intense form will fall upon the Jew, though "all the world" (Revelation 3:10) will come under the stroke. The God-fearing remnant, owned here as "My people", are called upon to hide themselves during that terrible period, and this anticipates the fuller instructions given by the Lord in Matthew 24:15-21.

The severity of that hour and its world-wide effects are stated in the last verse of our chapter. For well-nigh two thousand years the Lord has been *in His place of mercy* towards rebellious man. Then it is said, "The Lord cometh *out of His place to punish*", not the Jew only but "the inhabitants of the earth" generally. Judgment is spoken of as His "strange" work, but it will come to pass in its season, and we must never forget it. Israel's revival will take place when the tribulation is over. The believer today may look to be taken out of the very "hour" of the coming tribulation, according to Revelation 3:10.

## CHAPTER 27

Chapter 27 continues the theme in somewhat poetic language. Note how four times is repeated the phrase "In that day". Judgment in the first place will reach the evil power that lies beneath the restless "sea" of nations. This "dragon" that is in the sea can be no other than Satan, and Revelation 20 reveals how he will be dealt with. Then at last Israel will be no longer a fruitless vine but rather "A vineyard of red wine." Then peace will ensue and Israel will be like a tree that is full of blossom, and fill the face of the world with fruit; becoming what God from the outset intended them to be. This will never come to pass as the result of their efforts. They will have to fulfil what is said at the beginning of verse 5, "let him take hold of My strength".

Verses 7-11 however, show that this desirable end will only be reached when God brings to a finish His governmental judgments upon that people. There is "the iniquity of Jacob" which will have to be purged from them by these severe dealings from the hand of God. Yet, even so, the smitings that will fall upon them will not reach the severity of those that will be visited upon the nations who smote them. Upon these there will fall unsparing judgment, but for Jacob the smitings will reach to the altars and groves and sun-images which shall be ground to powder. Thus the very judgments that God will inflict upon His people, largely by the hand of other people, will have the effect of destroying the very things that had been a snare to them.

In verse 12 we meet with the phrase "In that day" for the third time. There is to be once more a gathering of His people from the land of Egypt, but this time in a very different way. Then Moses brought them out in their thousands as a nation, but in the coming day it will be an individual matter. One by one they will be put right with God, and so gathered to the place of blessing.

But verse 13 declares that in that day, though there must be the individual work indicated, there will be great publicity about it. The "great trumpet" shall sound, announcing this mighty work of God, as also our Lord Himself declared in Matthew 24:31. Publicly the house of Jacob has been disciplined and overthrown through the long and weary centuries: as publicly shall they be recovered, restored and blessed, when God's work with them and in them is brought to completion. Then at last in the holy mount at Jerusalem they shall give to the Lord that worship which is His due. What a day that will be!

But how privileged are we, Christians, who may worship God revealed as Father, while praise is still silent in Zion. We worship today in spirit and in truth; presently God will be addressed as "Thou that inhabitest the praises of Israel" (Psalm 22:3).

# Chapters 28:1 — 35:10

## CHAPTER 28

Having recorded this prediction of the gathering from lands of affliction to Jerusalem of a remnant who shall worship the Lord there, the prophet again reverted to the denunciation of the existing state of the people. And first Ephraim, that is, the ten tribes, came before him — verses 1-13. They were debased as drunkards and yet wore pride as a crown. Against them the Lord would bring "a mighty and strong one", like a devastating storm or flood — doubtless the Assyrian army.

Yet, even so, there should be found a "residue of His people" who should have not a crown of pride but a crown of glory, in the Lord Himself. Though the mass of the people had "erred through wine" and they "stumble in judgment", these should be like little children, who learn a little at a time, step by step.

The prophet goes on to show that, though God might condescend to deal in this simple way with the mass of the people, even using "stammering lips and another tongue", yet they refuse to hear and are broken. The Apostle Paul refers to this passage in 1 Corinthians 14:21-22, to show that tongues are a sign to unbelievers rather than believers.

Then, at verse 14, the prophetic message turns from Ephraim to the scornful men who were ruling the two tribes from Jerusalem. They had made covenants and formed alliances and thus felt independent of God. Their alliance with some worldly power or powers — Egypt probably — was really an agreement with death and hell. It was all falsehood and would not stand. What would stand would be God's own work to be accomplished in the coming Messiah.

Verse 16 is quoted by the Apostle Peter in his first epistle (2:6) and Paul alludes to it in Romans 10:11. Old Jacob, when dying, alluded to Christ as "the Stone of Israel" (Genesis 49:24) and here also He is viewed in connection with Israel. In Peter we discover that what will be true for them in the day to come has an application to us today. The Christ was indeed *tried* at His first advent, and revealed as the *sure* foundation, and though He is not yet manifested as the *corner* stone, His preciousness is the portion of those who believe, as Peter tells us. Hence we shall not "make haste", in alarm or confusion — the New Testament rendering of this word is "ashamed", and "confounded". Note too that this wonderful Stone is laid in Zion which is symbolic of God acting in His mercy.

But while mercy brings a solid foundation in blessing for the believer, it involves judgment for the unbeliever, as the subsequent verses show. "I will appoint judgment for a line, and righteousness for a plummet" (New Trans.), and this results in the hail of God's judgment sweeping away the refuges of lies and the covenants with death that men make. This came to pass for Israel shortly after Isaiah's day, and it will come to pass on a world-wide scale at the end of this age, though judgment is declared to be God's "strange work" (verse 21).

The latter verses of our chapter speak thus of the unsparing judgments of God, described as "a consumption, even determined upon the whole earth", so they are not to be confined to Israel. This shows indeed that the end of the age is mainly in view, and the figure used in verses 23-29 indicates that the harvest of judgment to be reaped is the result of the ploughing and sowing that has preceded it on man's part.

## CHAPTER 29

Chapter 29 continues this solemn strain. The city where David dwelt was once Ariel, meaning "The lion of God", but it was to be brought low. Though Hezekiah, a godly king, was either on the throne or shortly to ascend it, the state of the people was as described in verses 9-13. Their eyes were closed to God and to His word. Neither the learned nor the unlearned had any reference to His word, and any fear Godward that possessed them was taught "by the precept of men". Consequently their religion was mere lip-profession without heart-reality, and therefore offensive to God. No wonder that judgment came from the hand of God.

And thus it always must be. We find the Apostle Paul alluding to this scripture in Acts 13:41, for he spoke of prophets — in the plural — and so he did not only have Habakkuk 1:5 in his mind. If men close their eyes against the light and turn things upside down, they have to reap the fruit of their ways. How much of today's religion is just a matter of drawing near to God with the mouth while the heart is far away from Him? Let each of us judge ourselves as to this matter.

Though judgment against Ariel was executed soon after Isaiah's day, yet the terms of the prophecy go far beyond that, for the destruction of her foes is plainly announced in verse 7, and again at the end of the chapter. The adversary will be judged, and those amongst themselves who were watching for iniquity and making a man an offender for a word will be cut off. This will only come to pass at the end of the age, and then the name of the God of Israel will be feared and sanctified, and those that erred shall be rightly taught.

## CHAPTER 30

But at the moment the people had to be called "rebellious children" (30:1), and the prophet recurs to what they were doing at that time. He said of them, "who take counsel, but not of Me, and who make leagues, but not by My Spirit" (New Trans.). They were relying on Egypt, instead of turning to the Lord, and they are plainly told that Egypt would be a shame and a reproach instead of any profit to them. In the New Translation the latter part of verse 7 runs, "therefore have I named her, Arrogance, that doeth nothing"; with a note that the word used is "Rahab", which has that meaning.

This was bad enough, but in the succeeding verses we get something worse. The people would not hear the word of the Lord. True prophecy they would not tolerate. They wanted, and would only listen to, "smooth" things, even if they were "deceits". Words that were "right", they refused. So when the Lord said that they would be saved in returning to Him and resting in Him, and that their strength would consequently be found in quietness and confidence in Him, they said, No. They preferred to flee upon horses — for which Egypt was famous. As a result, judgment should fall.

This reliance upon Egypt was specially offensive to God, since from that very people He had delivered them by His judgments at the start of their national history. It is equally offensive to God if the Christian, who has been delivered from the world-system and its coming judgment, goes back to it, relying on its power or its wisdom, instead of finding his resource in God as emergencies arise. Egypt had its *pleasures* and its *treasures*, from which Moses turned, and they typify the things which are *not* for the believer.

In verse 18 of our chapter a different note is sounded, which continues to the end. The Lord speaks of mercy that shall yet be shown to them, since He delights in it. Just when everything seems lost, and they are left as a lonely "beacon upon the top of a mountain", mercy will be shown; and as we read these verses (18-33) we see that though the Lord will afflict them in His holy government, yet He will ultimately guide them, so that when they might turn aside to the right hand or the left, He will say, "This is the way, walk ye in it". Then they will cast away the idols that once they loved.

Prosperity will then set in, but the details of verses 25 and 26 go far beyond anything yet realized, and therefore look on to the last days. So also the tremendous judgments upon the nations, of verses 28 and 30, which will make the song to rise and the holy solemnity to be kept in the mountain of the Lord, who will be known as "the Mighty one [Rock] of Israel."

The closing verses are remarkable. Tophet was a valley close to Jerusalem, defiled by horrible heathen practices (see, 2 Kings 23:10; Jeremiah 7:31-32), so that it becomes a symbol of fiery judgment. Not only will the Assyrian be cast there but also "for the king it is prepared". Who this "king" may be is not specified, but doubtless he is that wilful king of whom Daniel 11:36 speaks, and whom we identify with the second "beast" of Revelation 13; that one who will come in his own name, as the Lord Jesus predicted in John 5:43, and who will be received by apostate Jews as their king. He will be the foe within, as the Assyrian the foe without. The doom of both is fixed.

## CHAPTER 31

In chapter 31 the prophet returns to the denunciation of his own people who were turning to Egypt. From a political standpoint it doubtless seemed a prudent thing to do. But it involved turning away from God — leaning upon the material and ignoring the spiritual. This is a very easy thing to do, and it is far less excusable in us than it was in them. Alas, how often have we done something similar! But, in spite of this defection on their part, the Lord was not going utterly to forsake them, as verses 4 and 5 show. Hence the invitation to turn to the Lord and cast away their idols, which lay at the root of all the trouble. If they did this, the Lord would intervene on their behalf and the Assyrian be destroyed.

## CHAPTER 32

But how should all this be accomplished? Chapter 32 furnishes the answer: God's King would appear, reigning in righteousness, and a new order of things be established. We are carried back in thought to chapter 11, where Christ was presented as the "Shoot" out of Jesse in His Manhood, and as the "Root" out of which Jesse sprang as to His Deity. He is to be King, and in verse 2 His Manhood is specially emphasised, befitting the fact that as King He is characterized by the seven-fold Spirit of Jehovah, of whom He is the visible Representative.

This world has indeed been swept by tempests of Satanic power, since he is "the prince of the power of the air". In spite of all man's cleverness it has proved itself to be "a dry place", devoid of real refreshment, and also "a weary land", where men spend their lives chasing what proves to be emptiness. The futility of Man's efforts is being manifested daily, and the cry from many may be summarized as "Wanted a man!" Satan's man will first appear, bringing evil to a climax, but to be destroyed by the Man of God's purpose, who will fulfil this word. He will introduce the three things indicated — *salvation, satisfaction,* and *re-invigoration* in a land no longer weary but rather restful.

If verse 2 gives a lovely picture of what Christ in kingly power will be, verses 3 and 4 reveal that there will be a work wrought in the souls of those who will enter these millennial scenes and enjoy the blessedness of the reign of Christ. They will have become a people of clear vision, of opened ears, of understanding hearts, and of plain and forceful speech. Observe the order. It is just the same today. First, apprehension; then, heart understanding; and lastly, the plain expression of what is believed, for out of the abundance of the heart the mouth speaketh.

But the fact that grace will so work in the hearts of some must make more manifest the evil that will still control many others, and of this the succeeding verses speak. Other scriptures show us that such will come under judgment and not enter the kingdom.

In view of these predictions the prophet now makes an appeal to the people of his own day, addressing it to those on whom the lesser responsibility rests. The men of the nation were mainly responsible, but the women too were careless and ease-loving, and upon them also the sorrows would fall until God intervened, not only by Christ, the King reigning in righteousness, but also by the outpouring of the Spirit from on high, of which Joel in his prophecy speaks more specifically.

Thus in this chapter we have brought together both what will be established externally by Christ as King and Saviour, and what will be wrought internally by the poured-out Spirit. Then indeed peace, quietness and assurance for ever will be reached as the work and effect of righteousness. These things men are seeking today, but they have not got the secure basis on which they can be established. They will come in the future age, but while we wait for that, we who believe enjoy them in a spiritual and individual way, through the faith of the work of Christ and in the power of the indwelling Spirit of God.

Israel will know these things even when judgment falls on others, as verse 19 indicates; and with that assurance the seeds of truth may be sown and cultivated "beside all waters" with confidence in the ultimate result.

## CHAPTER 33

Chapters 33, 34 and 35 all have the same general themes: God's judgments on Israel's foes; His disciplinary dealings with His people, leading them ultimately to look to Him; then their blessing under His hand. Let us observe in brief detail how these things are presented.

First, a woe is pronounced against some people who treacherously aim at spoiling the people; and this leads in verse 2 to a touching prayer for the intervention of the Lord, when He will be exalted, and salvation and stability will come to pass. Yet the desolations of verse 8 will precede this, and when a wilderness has been created, Jehovah will rise up and be exalted in judging the foe. There may have been some fulfilment of all this soon after Isaiah's day, but the complete fulfilment waits for the end of the age, when there will arise a man of whom it can be said, "he hath broken the covenant ... he regardeth no man" (verse 8). There will be great antagonistic powers in the last days.

Then in verse 13 and onwards we learn what will be the effect of these judgments upon Israel themselves. They will have a winnowing effect, separating the ungodly from the righteous. Sinners will be found, even in Zion, as the result of their hypocrisy, but they will be exposed and be fearful of the fiery judgment; while the really godly, who walk in righteousness will dwell on high in security with necessities supplied; and moreover "the King in His beauty" will be before their eyes. The fierce people will have disappeared and they will meditate upon the terror that once held sway, when their resources had to be counted and weighed.

The chapter closes with a call to view Zion and Jerusalem as at last a city of unruffled peace, of unshaken stability. Jehovah will be to them as a broad, placid river, undisturbed by men's ships of war, which are all dispersed, according to verse 23. The lame take the prey; the inhabitants are saved from their iniquities and their sicknesses, since Jehovah is Judge, King and Saviour. We hardly need add that all this has never come to pass yet.

## CHAPTER **34**

Chapter 34 opens with a call to all the world to hearken, since all nations have to face the judgments of God, which will reach even to "the host of heaven", since there is to be that conflict in the heavens of which we read in Revelation 12:7-8; and as a result Satan will lose his foothold there and be confined in his fury to earth. But in a very special manner the sword of the Lord will come down upon Idumea; that is, upon Esau in his descendants, who are specially under the curse.

In the last Old Testament book we find God saying that He hated Esau; and one of the Minor Prophets, Obadiah, is entirely occupied with predictions against him. Here we find the same thing, and we are told in verse 8 that vengeance falls upon them in recompence for "the controversy of Zion." In Zion God elected to have mercy upon Jacob, whereas Edom pursued them with undying hatred, as we see in Psalm 83:3-6. In result, judgments of special severity will fall on the land of Idumea, and the rest of chapter 34 gives us the solemn details of it.

Preliminary movements, which will lead to all this, are taking place today. Israel now has a footing in their own land, yet among the thousands are but few "just and devout", as was Simeon of old. There are all too many "sinners in Zion" who would be afraid. The sons of Esau and Ishmael surround them in very antagonistic and aggressive mood. Who can tell what may *soon* happen? But we can tell from this scripture what will *ultimately* come to pass, and how God will intervene in judgment.

## CHAPTER 35

The Divine intervention having taken place, the blessing for Israel and the land, predicted in chapter 35, will be brought to pass. The picture is a lovely one — a delightful scene of earthly blessing. The curse of Genesis 3:17-18 will be lifted, so that the very deserts will be abundantly fruitful. The vengeance of God will mean deliverance for Israel, and safety. But not only that, since they themselves will be transformed. They will see spiritually, they will hear, they will sing with gladness, and all their hopes be realized.

The figure in verse 7 is a striking one, for the word translated "parched ground" really means a "mirage"; the strange appearance of what looks like a lake in some dry region, but which is only an illusion. The illusion that poor Israel has pursued, while away from God, will cease, and a real lake of refreshment take its place. We may well use the same figure in the Gospel today, since men are chasing after an illusory satisfaction and joy in a variety of ways, while abiding satisfaction is only found in Christ.

Verse 8 emphasises holiness, which must ever mark the presence of God, and the way of holiness may be trodden by the humblest of men, who would be accounted a fool by worldly standards. We may thank God that it is so.

The description of blessedness ends with the alluring picture presented in verse 10. Those who enter into the everlasting joy and gladness will be the ransomed of the Lord. We can rejoice today in this forecast of the blessedness of the earthly Zion, while we remember with gladness that we are blessed "with all spiritual blessings in heavenly places in Christ" (Ephesians 1:3). And "the heavens are higher than the earth", as Isaiah himself presently reminds us.

# Chapters 36:1 — 40:8

After the lovely picture of blessedness on earth in the millennial age, presented to us in chapter 35, there is a break in the prophecy. The four chapters, 36-39, give us details of history in Hezekiah's reign, which are recounted also in 2 Kings, chapters 18-20, and again more briefly in 2 Chronicles 32.

Remembering that we have no *needless* repetitions in Scripture, we may ask why these chapters should be inserted here? The answer, we think, is twofold.

First, the personal piety of Hezekiah is recorded, so different from the state of the nation at large as depicted in the earlier chapters, and particularly chapter 1; and then how God answered his faith in the destruction of the Assyrian. Second, though his faith and dependence on God was so genuine, and his prayer for recovery so strikingly answered, these very mercies led to his failure in the matter of the Babylonian envoys which is recorded. This indicated that the more immediate judgments already pronounced could not be delayed.

## CHAPTER 37

## CHAPTER 36

Chapter 36 records in detail the arguments by which the herald of the king of Assyria tried to persuade the people of Jerusalem to an immediate surrender, and we must remember that about eight years previously Samaria had fallen before the Assyrian power, and later the defended cities of Judah had also fallen. So humanly speaking the position of Jerusalem was hopeless.

Rabshakeh's words were very specious. He knew the weakness of Egypt, in which the Jews were inclined to trust, as verse 6 shows; and as to which the people had already been warned by Isaiah. He completely mistook, however, Hezekiah's action in destroying the high places, for this, instead of being an offence against the Lord, was entirely in obedience to His word in Deuteronomy 12:1-6. So many previous kings, even the good ones, had overlooked this commandment of the Lord, but Hezekiah had been obedient and faithful.

Moreover, Rabshakeh falsely asserted that the Lord had told the Assyrian king to destroy Jerusalem, and then he appealed against Hezekiah to the citizens within hearing, for he evidently had a shrewd knowledge of their idolatrous tendencies, so different to their King. Many of them were secretly trusting in false gods and not in the Lord, so the reminder of the fact that the gods of many other cities had failed to deliver, was calculated to have weight in their minds. Still Hezekiah's command to the men to keep silence prevailed, and they answered him not a word.

## CHAPTER 37

Eliakim, of whom we read in chapter 22, with others brought news of all this to Hezekiah, and his reaction to it is found in the first five verses of chapter 37. God was first in his thoughts, for covered with sackcloth, indicating sorrow and humiliation, he "went into the house of the Lord."

Then, in the second place, he turned to the prophet, through whom God had been speaking, confessing the low estate of himself and his people. He spoke of them as "the remnant that is left." He recognized the unity of all Israel. Now that the ten tribes had been deported, he did not fall into the snare of assuming that the two, over whom he was king, were more than a "remnant", left by the mercy of God. Much of the professing church today has been by the adversary deported from their true place and portion, so let any who have escaped this, and remain in any degree true to their original calling, never forget they have no other status than a remnant of the whole. They are not reconstituted as a separate entity.

Isaiah's response was one of assurance. God would deal with Sennacherib, firstly by causing him to hear a report as to the king of Ethiopia, lastly by death in his own land, and in between by the destruction of his boasted and apparently invincible army, of which we read at the end of the chapter.

Though not for the moment attacking Jerusalem, Sennacherib sent a further boastful message to Hezekiah — verses 10-13 — and Hezekiah's response follows. Instead of replying to man, he turned to God, spreading the letter before Him. In his prayer he acknowledged the military might of the Assyrian king, yet asked for deliverance on the ground that the Assyrian had sent "to reproach the living God."

This brought forth God's immediate answer through Isaiah, accepting the Assyrian challenge, which was not only reproachful but blasphemous also. The Assyrian would become a laughing-stock to Jerusalem. His earlier successes against other cities had been ordained of God; now turning against God, he would be utterly crushed, and the remnant of Judah should be delivered for the time being. The city should be spared for the Lord's own sake, as well as for David's sake.

The chapter closes with a brief record of the drastic smiting of the Assyrian army. No record of this has been found among the dug-up remains of Assyrian libraries and monuments, we understand; and no wonder! These ancient monarchs no more desired to keep their defeats and abasements in the memory of their public than the men of today. Sennacherib himself came to an ignominious end, as the last verse of our chapter declares.

## CHAPTER 38

And then, "In those days", just when Hezekiah had been so marvellously lifted up by this Divinely-wrought deliverance, he was smitten with an illness that brought him face to face with death. Through Isaiah, who just before had given him the message of deliverance for his city and people, he was told to prepare for his end. Unlike Asa, one of his predecessors, who when diseased "sought not to the Lord, but to the physicians", he did go straight to the Lord and with tears besought for his life. He was heard and 15 further years were granted to him.

He asked for a sign that he should recover, as the last verse of the chapter tells us, and a remarkable sign was given. That the shadow on the sun-dial should go ten degrees *backward* was entirely *contrary to nature*, but it was a sign befitting the fact that God was about to *reverse* Hezekiah's sickness, so that *contrary to the nature* of his disease, it should end in life and not death. A plaister of figs does not usually cure a virulently septic boil, but it did in this case as an act of God.

Unbelievers may of course refuse this story of the sun-dial incident, just as they do the incident of the long day, recorded in Joshua 10:13, when the apparent course of the sun was arrested. It is worthy of note that in Joshua the sun, "hasted not to go down *about a whole day*." The ten degrees of Hezekiah's time may have *completed* a whole day. He who established the course of the solar system can accelerate or retard it, if it pleases Him so to do.

The Apostle Paul has told us, in Romans 5:3-5, what excellent results in the hearts and lives of saints are produced by *tribulation*, since it leads to the in-shining of the love of God in the power of the Holy Spirit. A faint foreshadowing of this we find in the writing of Hezekiah after he was recovered — which writing is preserved for us in verses 10-20.

It begins on notes of great *mournfulness*, occupying five verses, but it ends on *songs* which are to fill the rest of his life. The change of tone begins when he recognized the affliction as coming from the hand of God. Moreover he discovered, as verse 16 shows, that what threatened death to his body brought life to his spirit, which is more important than the body.

Verse 17 too is full of instruction. It expresses what unconverted folk have sometimes found, as well as saints, when deeply tried or near to death. Hezekiah did not *then* concern himself with "my kingdom", or "my wealth", but "*my soul*". He also become conscious of "*my sins*", and that there was a "*pit of corruption*" into which his sins threatened to cast his soul. This must have been a very acute spiritual experience for him; and so it is equally for us.

But on the other hand he made some very joyous discoveries. First, he discovered that on God's part there was

"*love* to my soul", though he could not have known that
with the fulness that has only been revealed in Christ. Yet
it led to the further discovery that God had dealt with his
sins, though he could not have known that with the final-
ity that the Gospel brings to us. In his day there was "the
remission [i.e. passing over] of sins that are past" (Romans
3:25); that is, the sins of saints who lived before full
atonement was made by Christ on the cross. Still he knew
that God had cast all his sins *behind His back*; and since
God does not move in circles but rather straight forward
through the eternal ages, what He casts behind His back
is there for ever, and not as He said to Ephraim in Hosea
7:2, "before My face."

Consequently he had the happy assurance that *his soul was
delivered* from the doom that threatened it. The pit of corruption he would never see. What a wonderful experience
was brought to Hezekiah by this violent sickness! Since his
day many a saint has found a period of sickness, or of loss
in other ways, to be an occasion of rich spiritual gain;
many a sinner has been laid low to be broken in spirit and
humbled for eternal blessing.

But, before we leave this chapter, there is another sobering
reflection; for 2 Kings 21:1 reveals that his son Manasseh,
who succeeded him, was only 12 years old when he began
to reign; that is, he was born after Hezekiah's recovery, as
the result of his added 15 years of life. And this Manasseh
reigned for 55 years and did such evil in and with the
nation that the Babylonian captivity had to be inflicted
upon them, as is shown so plainly in 2 Kings 21:10-16.
Let us learn from this that we may earnestly beseech God
for something that we regard as a favour, and it may be
granted us, and yet we may have subsequently to discover
that the "favour" we demanded carried with it consequences that were by no means favourable.

## CHAPTER 39

And this reflection is deepened when we read chapter 39. The Assyrian having been smitten of God, the revived city of Babylon began to lift up its head, though more than a century had to pass before it became the predominant power. Hezekiah had been magnified in the sight of surrounding peoples by the miraculous destruction of the Assyrian army, and also by his own miraculous recovery; hence the complimentary embassage from Merodach-baladan, which pleased him much and led to a display of his pride.

We are told quite definitely in 2 Chronicles 32:25, 26, and 31 that God's kind deliverances led to the heart of Hezekiah being lifted up with pride, and that God permitted the testing of these men from Babylon to "try him", and to "know all that was in his heart." The Babylonians, whether they knew it or not, set a trap, and into it he fell, displaying for his own glory all that God had permitted him to acquire. Hence the solemn message Isaiah had to bring him, of coming judgment from Babylon on his sons and people.

Nor does the last verse of our chapter present Hezekiah to us in a very favourable light. He evidently cared much more for his own personal success and comfort than for the welfare of his posterity or of his nation. He had been favoured of God, but he passes from our view too much wrapped up in his own blessings, too little concerned for others on whom the judgment was to fall.

Thus these four historical chapters, whilst recording God's merciful intervention both for the nation and for Hezekiah personally, show us quite plainly that there was nothing in the people nor in the best of their kings that would avert the more immediate judgment on Jerusalem, that in the earlier chapters Isaiah had foretold.

## CHAPTER 40

We might therefore have expected that chapter 40 would commence on a mournful note, calling for misery and tears rather than comfort. But no, "Comfort ye, comfort ye My people, saith your God"; and that in view of the main theme, which is developed in the remaining chapters. In the earlier portion — chapters 1–35 — the main theme has been the *sinful state* of both Israel and the surrounding nations, and God's judgments upon them all, though relieved by happy references to Messiah's kingdom and glory, as in chapters 9, 11, 28, 32. Now, though God's controversy with Israel still continues, both as to their idolatry and their rejection of their Messiah, it is *His advent*, both in suffering and in glory, that is the main theme.

Comfort, then, is now pronounced and offered to God's people and, as to the immediate context, it is based upon the declaration in verse 2. It is not that their iniquity is condoned or made light of but rather that its "double", or *appropriate punishment*, has been exacted, and thus it has been pardoned, and the time of "warfare", or suffering, is over. The verse does not state how this "double" from the Lord's hand has been received.

The explanation of it lies in the subsequent chapters. As to the government of God, operating in this world, they receive it to the full in heavy chastisement, as indicated in chapters 57, 58 and 59. As to the more serious matter of God's eternal judgment on sin, they receive it in the vicarious sufferings of their Messiah and Saviour, whom once they rejected. This we see in chapter 53, where we find them saying prophetically, "The chastisement of our peace was upon Him", since "The Lord hath laid on Him the iniquity of us all."

So verse 3 presents us with that which the Evangelist Mark has declared to be, "The beginning of the gospel of Jesus Christ, the Son of God": — the mission of John the Baptist. The prophecy here is quite unmistakable for John himself claimed to be "the voice"; as recorded in John 1:23. Equally unmistakable is the true greatness and glory of the One that he announced; for it was "Jehovah" and "our God" for whom he prepared the way.

The language of verse 4 is figurative but the meaning is plain, and in keeping with the words of the virgin Mary recorded in Luke 1:52. John's baptism was one of repentance, and that brings all men down to a common level of lowliness and self-judgment. The Pharisees saw this clearly enough and it was the reason why they, being puffed up with pride, "rejected the counsel of God against themselves, being not baptized of him" (Luke 7:30).

But though the allusion to John is so plain, verse 5 carries us on to what will be fulfilled at the second coming of Christ. The glory of the Lord was indeed revealed at His first coming, and it proved to be "the glory as of the Only Begotten of the Father" (John 1:14). But in the same verse we read, "*We* beheld His glory", and the context of these words shows that the mass of the people did not behold it. The disciples were the exception to the rule. Not until His second advent comes to pass will "all flesh" see it. Revelation 1:7 declares the publicity of His second advent.

So the prophecy here, as is usual in the Old Testament, has both advents in view. The same feature meets us in chapter 61:2, for, when the Lord Jesus read this in the synagogue at Nazareth, He stopped in the middle of the verse, knowing that the latter part of it referred to His second advent in power and not His first advent in grace. A *single* star shines in our night sky but when seen through a telescope it proves to be *two*. So this predicted advent of Jehovah in the person of the Messiah is discovered to be two advents in the clearer light of the New Testament.

But the immediate effect of the presence of the Lord and the revelation of His glory would be — What? The complete exposure of the sinfulness and frailty of mankind. Not merely Gentile flesh, or depraved flesh, but *"all flesh"* is as withered and worthless grass. The Apostle Peter quotes these words at the end of the first chapter of his first Epistle, but in contrast therewith he dwells upon the word of our God which stands for ever. And he assures us that by that living and abiding word of God we have been "born again". So once more we see how New Testament grace shines above Old Testament law.

## Chapters 40:9 — 45:14

In spite of the fact that the revelation of the glory of the Lord brings to light, as nothing else does, the sinfulness and frailty of man, there is also brought "good tidings", and this it is which furnishes the "comfort" for "My people". Zion and Jerusalem are represented as lifting up the voice and saying to the cities of Judah, "Behold your God!"

About the sixth hour on the day of the crucifixion Pilate brought forth Jesus, and said to the crowd in Jerusalem, "Behold your King!" (John 19:14). This provoked the violent cry, "Away with Him, crucify Him." In our Scripture the prophet sees the same wonderful Person, but coming in the splendour of Deity with "strong hand". This will be good tidings indeed, after the painful display of sin and utter weakness on the part of men.

It is the Lord Jehovah who is coming with might, but it is "His Arm" who will rule for Him. As we go through these later chapters of Isaiah we shall find the Lord Jesus presented as the Arm of Jehovah some ten or twelve times. In this character He is seen as the One who executes in power all the will and purpose of Jehovah. He is also presented as the "Servant", who is to carry out the yet more wonderful work of sin-bearing and suffering. In the passages that speak of Him as the Servant we see predictions that view Him in His first advent in grace: in those that present Him as the "Arm" our thoughts are carried on to His second advent in glory.

It is so here in verse 10. The Arm is going to *rule* for Jehovah, rather than suffer for Him. He will dispense reward and recompence to others in the day of His glory; and at the same time He will be a tender Shepherd to those who are His flock, gathering even the lambs to His bosom. In other words, while ruling in power at His second advent, He will display to His own all the grace which shone forth in Him at His first advent. As we look abroad in the earth today, we see how badly needed is the ruling power of a strong hand, and men desire to grasp that power so as to rule in their own interests. The Arm of Jehovah will rule "for Him"; and what a day that will be when the will of God will be done on earth as it is in heaven!

The verses that follow present to us the greatness and glory of the Creator-God in the most exalted language. So great is He that the mighty oceans lie in the hollow of His hand like a few drops of water; the expanse of the heavens, illimitable to us, is but the span of His hand; the dust of the earth as well as the mountains and hills are but small things, weighed in His scales. As to understanding, the Spirit of the Lord is far above taking any counsel from man.

We live in a day when nations are rising up and asserting themselves, and arming to the hilt, in order to enforce their will. What are they in the presence of God? They are like a small drop which may hang on a finger-tip, when taken out of a bucket of water; or like the small dust left on the scales when the substance weighed therein has been removed — so insignificant that no one pays attention to it. The nations that look so imposing and threatening to us, are counted by Him as "less than nothing, and vanity." It is good for us to measure them by God's standards and not by our own.

God then is great beyond all our thoughts, as verse 18 indicates, and in the presence of His glory how foolish and contemptible, as verses 19 and 20 say, are the makers of graven images that have not even the power of motion. And further, how feeble and insignificant are men, who appear but as grasshoppers, and their princes and judges but as nothing and vanity, and as stubble in the face of a whirlwind. We may also lift up our eyes and behold the mighty creation outside our little earth; all numbered and named by Him, and upheld by Him too, so that not one fails. He who created them has no equal and cannot be likened to any other. We do well to ponder this magnificent passage, for this God of ineffable power and majesty has been made known to us in Christ as our Father.

The closing verses of the chapter, while not revealing Him as Father, do make known His care and support for those who trust in Him. Where all human power fails He gives strength to those who express their trust by waiting upon Him. As they wait their strength is renewed, and granted as it is needed. Some may need the strength that elevates; others the strength that runs the errands appointed of God, and others again that which enables for the steady and continuous walk through life for the pleasure of God. As we wait on God each shall receive the needed strength. The greatness of our God, as well as His goodness, is the guarantee of it.

## CHAPTER 41

In view of this disclosure of the glory of God a call goes out to all mankind as chapter 41 opens — for the word "people" in verse 1 should really be in the plural "peoples". God will reason with them as to His governmental ways in the earth. Verse 2 mentions a king, coming from the east of Palestine, who should be a conqueror, ruling over kings. It seems that this is a prophecy as regards the day in which Isaiah wrote, and was fulfilled in Cyrus, who is named in the verse that opens chapter 45. God raises up whom He pleases to carry out His designs in the earth. In contrast with this men in their folly and blindness manufacture their idols, as stated in verses 6 and 7. This controversy with Israel as to their persistent turning to idols continues till we reach the end of chapter 48.

In verses 8 and 9 of our chapter Israel is reminded that as the seed of Abraham, who is honoured as "My friend", they are a chosen people and called to be the *servant* of God. How foolish then this turning to idols! And in the succeeding verses we find the most assuring words of encouragement and support which, if only received in faith, would have lifted them far above any reliance on idolatrous things. They should be upheld and their enemies confounded. The Holy One of Israel would be their Redeemer, and make them like a threshing instrument scattering their foes. Moreover He would be as a fountain of water to them, meeting all their needs.

In the light of this comes the challenge to the idols and their followers. Let them produce their cause; let them foretell the future and "declare things for to come." This they could not do, and an abomination were they and their votaries. A further reference to the coming conqueror from the north-east is found in verses 25 and 26, and the chapter closes with words of contempt for the men who supported the idols and the counsels they gave.

## CHAPTER 42

This throws into relief the opening of chapter 42, where the prophecy turns from Israel, as the failing servant of God, to introduce the Lord Jesus as the true Servant of God. Our attention is to be fixed on Him for He is the chosen One in whom the delight of God rests. He it is who will bring forth judgment for the nations, and not only for Israel. Here again we find a prophecy which was fulfilled in part at His first advent, but awaits His second advent for the fulfilment of other details.

The prophecy is quoted in Matthew 12:14-21 as showing the lowliness and forbearance of His coming in grace. The Pharisees were indeed as unreliable and worthless as a bruised reed, and as objectionable as smoking flax, yet He neither broke nor quenched them. He was not an agitator, inflaming the multitude. The powers that were against Him were calculated to make any servant of God be discouraged and fail, yet He carried on His service to the end. He brought forth judgment according to truth by His sacrificial death and resurrection, though we must wait for the second coming to see the public establishment of judgment in the earth, so that the most distant isle shall wait for His law.

Our attention having been called to this true Servant, we have in verses 5-9 words prophetically addressed to Him. In verse 5 the acts of God in creation are stressed. Not only are the heavens and the earth the work of His hands but mankind also. He has given us not only the breath of our bodies but also the spirit, that is man's distinguishing feature in contrast to the beasts. Now this mighty Creator has called His true Servant in righteousness and established Him as a *covenant* to the people and a light to the nations. In verse 9 Jehovah is presented as declaring *new* things, so we may discern that the *new covenant* is predicted here, though not stated with the fulness found in Jeremiah 31.

We may note that Ezekiel 36 predicts the *new birth*, which is needed if the blind eyes are to be opened, as in verse 7 of our chapter, to "see the kingdom of God" (John 3:3); whilst in Jeremiah we have predicted the *new covenant*, under which the kingdom will be established. In Isaiah we have many of the *new things* predicted, that will mark the kingdom when it is finally established under the rule of Christ.

These new things will move those who enter into them to "Sing unto the Lord a *new song*"; and the thought, of how the glory of the Lord will be manifested and His praise be sung, fills verses 10-12. But the next verses show that what will bring blessing to His people will mean judgment and destruction to His foes. While the call will come to many who once were deaf and blind, that they may hear and see, the folly and judgment of those who turned to idols will be revealed.

The chapter closes with an appeal to those of Isaiah's day in view of these things. Israel had been called as God's servant and should have been a messenger to the nations on His behalf, yet they had been blind in all essential things. As to privilege they were "perfect"; as to their moral state they were blind. Still, as verse 21 indicates, God is not thereby defeated. His righteousness will be established and His law magnified and made honourable — doubtless in connection with His true Servant. But for the present all was failure on the part of Israel and consequently they were spoiled and robbed, and the law dishonoured by their disobedience.

## Chapter 43

We might have expected therefore that chapter 43 would have contained further warnings and judgments; but it opens rather on a note of grace. The Apostle Peter wrote to the scattered Jewish believers of his day how "the prophets have inquired and searched diligently, who prophesied of the grace that should come unto you", which grace meant "salvation" (1 Peter 1:10); and here is a case in point. In the presence of their evil, God falls back upon His original purpose and His redeeming work. Redemption by power was what the people looked for, and was mainly the theme here, as the succeeding verses show; but presently there will come before us the far deeper work of the suffering Servant — redemption by blood.

The whole chapter is characterized by two things. First, by the declaration of what God will do in His sovereign mercy for His poor blind and deaf people, who were set up to be His witnesses to the other nations. He will bring down their foes, be they Babylon and the Chaldeans or other peoples, and He will deal with their sins, as indicated in verse 25. How He will do this in righteousness is not revealed in this chapter; but the result will be that this people whom He had formed for Himself will ultimately show forth His praise, as stated in verse 21.

But second, though all this grace is so strikingly promised, the existing state of the people in rebellion and sin is not glossed over. They are again made to face their fallen state. There is the promise of a regathering of their seed from the east and west, from north and south, but at the moment they had turned from the Lord, as verse 22 says;

they did not honour Him with offerings and sacrifices, but wearied Him with their iniquities. As their first father — Adam — had sinned, so they had followed in his footsteps. Because of this the curse and reproach lay upon them, imposed by the hand of God.

## CHAPTER 44

But yet again, chapter 44 opens with a word of mercy. In spite of his crookedness Jacob was God's servant, chosen by Him, and God is always true to His purpose and able to carry it out. This fact should bring comfort and strength to every believer today. The history of the church, like that of Israel, is one of failure and departure from the Divine call and way, yet the purpose of God for us will stand no less securely than His purpose for Israel. The failure and sin is not excused, though in the presence of it the sovereign grace of God is magnified.

The first eight verses of this chapter breathe out that grace in no uncertain terms. The sovereignty of God is declared, for He is the First and He is the Last, and beside Him there is no "God", or, "Rock", as the margin reads. Consequently, though He will chastise in His holy government, He will ultimately bless according to His original purpose.

But at the time when Isaiah wrote there was among the people this persistent tendency to turn to their idols and false gods. Hence once more, in verses 9-20 of our chapter, God reasons with the people about their folly in this matter. The work of smith and carpenter are described, as a result of which an image is constructed, "according to the beauty of a man", which can be kept in the house. Then our thoughts are carried to the work of planting trees, or hewing them down, and then the absurdity of using some of the wood for warming oneself, or baking bread and roasting meat, and then out of the remainder fashioning a "god", before which one falls down and asks for deliverance!

The folly and absurdity of such doings should have been plain to all the people, but it was not. How was it that their eyes were closed and their understanding darkened? The trouble lay in their hearts, which were deceived. Hence they were unable to consider and discern the lie in their "right hand". The position today is just the same. Why do so many take up the erroneous religious cults that abound? The trouble lies not so much in their intellects as in their hearts. It is true for them as for Israel of old that "a deceived heart hath turned him aside".

Having thus reasoned with the people, once more the prophet announces the merciful interposition of God, both in its ultimate display, which is still future, and in its more immediate display in the raising up of an eastern monarch, who should be favourable to them. As to the future, they would yet be the servant of God, their transgressions and sins blotted out. This would be accomplished on the basis of redemption so that the very heavens as well as the earth will break into song, and the Lord Himself be glorified.

Then in the closing verses a deliverance that reached them about two centuries later is predicted, and Cyrus is named long before he was born. The statement that Jerusalem and the temple should be rebuilt clearly indicated that they should be destroyed, and this would confound the tokens of the lying diviners, who were always saying smooth and prosperous things, as other scriptures show. Judgment would fall, but mercy would in its season be shown, and the man through whom it would reach them is named.

## CHAPTER 45

In the opening verses of chapter 45 the prophet speaks to
Cyrus on God's behalf, though as yet he had no existence.
He was to be raised up as anointed for this particular service and his hand would be holden of God till it was
accomplished. The details given in verses 1-3 were strikingly fulfilled, as we find recorded in the book of Daniel,
though Darius the Mede is the conqueror mentioned
there. He was the commander of the Medo-Persian army,
but the rising power of Cyrus the Persian lay behind him.
As we read these verses, we see Belshazzar, and "the joints
of his loins were loosed, and his knees smote one against
another" (Daniel 5:6). We see the great gates of Babylon
open and broken; and then, as a result of the fall of the
great city, "the treasures of darkness, and hidden riches of
secret places" are in the hands of Cyrus. We see here an
allusion to the vessels of the house of the Lord, which
Nebuchadnezzar had carried to Babylon, being restored,
as recorded in Ezra 1:7-11.

Here then is a remarkable prophecy that was literally fulfilled within two hundred years of its utterance. God
called him by his name, and surnamed him, though Cyrus
had not known Him. Yet the words of the decree of
Cyrus, recorded in 2 Chronicles 36:23 and again in Ezra
1:2; would make it likely that in some way Isaiah's
prophecy was brought to his notice.

With Israel's persistent idolatry still in mind, Jehovah
declares in the succeeding verses His surpassing greatness.
All things are in His hands. He creates the light and the
darkness, the peace and the "evil", in the sense of disaster.
Man is but a potsherd of the earth — the broken piece of
a pot! Let man recognize his own littleness. Let him strive
with another potsherd like himself if he will, but let him
not strive with the Creator. It is not fitting that a man

should strive with his father or mother, much less with his Maker. Verses 5, 13 and 14 again refer to Cyrus and the way in which God would raise him up. It would be "in righteousness", for he would carry into effect the will of God; and to do the will of God is righteousness.

The raising up of Cyrus and the granting to him such wide dominion was a surprising act in view of the previous power and magnificence of Babylon. We need not wonder that it is claimed as a display of the surpassing power of God, in the presence of which idols are nothing.

## Chapters 45:14 — 49:4

The power of God, that, by the raising up of Cyrus, would accomplish His purpose to release those whom He calls "My captives", would only be perceived by faith. Therefore the prophet exclaims, "Verily Thou art a God that hidest Thyself". A servant of God has very truly and aptly remarked, "God's ways are behind the scenes, but He moves all the scenes which He is behind" {J.N.Darby}.

Men may act to achieve their own purposes without any thought of God and yet God may be behind their doings, overruling them to serve His own ends. Israel is to know God as Saviour and be delivered from their idols. This was in part accomplished when by the decree of Cyrus a remnant returned to their own land; for after that deliverance the demon of idolatry was cast out of them, and outwardly they served the God of their fathers. But the everlasting salvation mentioned in verse 17 is not yet theirs. Each "salvation" as yet granted to them has only lasted for a time. When it does come by the advent of Christ, it will abide "world without end", or, "to the ages of ages".

This promised salvation is guaranteed most solemnly in verses 18 and 19 by Jehovah Himself who is the Creator.

As Creator He had formed the earth for mankind to inhabit it. He did not create it "in vain", or "as waste"; an allusion doubtless to Genesis 1:2, where the earth was found in a condition described as "without form", or, "as waste"; the same expression being used there as here. When the earth, subsequent to its original creation, had become waste, He reduced it to form and order for the use of man. He who had done this now guaranteed salvation for Israel. He promised openly and in righteousness. This made it certain that the salvation when it arrived would be accomplished in a righteous way; just as the righteousness in which every believer now stands before God is brought to pass on a righteous basis.

So the call of God to the seed of Jacob had not been in vain. But not only Israel is in view but Gentiles also, as verse 20 shows. The call is to those that are "escaped of the nations", which shows that judgment will fall on the nations, and only those that escape it will enter into the blessing that is promised, just as it is only the remnant of Israel that will be saved. The nations had been full of idolatry, praying to "a god that cannot save", so they are called, that they may know a God who can save.

Verses 21-25 furnish a remarkable forecast of the Gospel, as it is unfolded in Romans 3. Against the dark background of idolatry the Lord presents Himself as "a just God and a Saviour". The law had revealed Him to Israel as a just God who judges all their ways. Only in the Gospel is He declared to be God who *saves* in righteousness. Christ has been "set forth … a propitiation through faith in His blood … to declare … at this time His righteousness; that He might be just, and the Justifier of him which believeth in Jesus" (Romans 3:25-26).

In our chapter, not only are justice and salvation brought together but faith is also indicated, though not mentioned, for the way in which the salvation is to become effective is stated as, "Look unto Me". No works of law are demanded but the look of faith, for beyond all contradiction in an emergency we look to someone in whom we believe, and hence in whom we trust. And again, the call goes out far beyond the bounds of Israel, for any to "the ends of the earth" may look and be saved. In Romans 3:21 this righteousness of God apart from the law is said to be "witnessed by the law and the prophets", and the verses we are considering are certainly one item of witness furnished by the prophets.

Verse 22 then conveys an invitation to faith, but verse 23 shows that God in His majesty must be acknowledged by all, though many may not have answered the invitation in faith. And how is this bowing of the knee and the swearing of the tongue to come to pass? Philippians 2:10-11 answers the question conclusively. The Person of the Godhead, to whom the obeisance and confession will be universally made, is no other than the Lord Jesus, who accomplished the righteousness by His obedience unto death. Righteousness and strength are found only in Him, and as the last verse says, it is "the seed of Israel" who will glory in Him as a justified people. Many who are "seed of Jacob" according to the flesh, are not "seed of Israel" according to God.

Before leaving this chapter notice how in the latter part of it the *exclusive claim* of Jehovah is emphasised again and again. Beside Him there is "none else". The faith of Christ, and the Gospel which proclaims it, have today just this exclusive claim, as witnessed in such scriptures as John 6:68; 14:6; Acts 4:12; Galatians 1:8-9. There are today men who would go to the Buddhist or Confucian acknowledging their religions as ways to God and only claiming that "Christianity" offers them a rather superior way. In so doing they bring themselves near to, if not actually under, the apostolic curse of Galatians 1:8, while they avoid the reproach that the Gospel brings. It is this exclusive claim, inherent in the Gospel, which provokes the opposition.

## CHAPTER 46

The opening verses of chapter 46 pick up the theme that runs through these chapters — that of the persistent idolatry of the people. Bel and Nebo were two of the idols of Babylon, and the prophet sees the images representing them placed upon beasts ready for flight, just as at the beginning of the last chapter he had seen Cyrus taking the city. The word translated "carriages" means "things lifted up to be carried", not the vehicle on which they are placed.

So verses 1 and 2 are really ironical. The heavy images were placed on the backs of oxen, that staggered and finally collapsed, unable to deliver the gods into safety. Bel and Nebo could not even deliver themselves; much less anyone who trusted in them!

Hence the appeal of verses 3 and 4. It is made, notice, to "the house of Jacob", in contrast to "the seed of Israel", mentioned previously, even if amongst them were to be found a remnant of the house of Israel. In contrast to the Babylonian gods that had to be borne on the backs of weary beasts so ineffectually, here is One who would support and carry, from their birth to the grey hairs of old age, those who trusted Him; One who would never let them down but deliver them. How great the contrast!

The contrast exists around us today. It is still a pertinent question — Do you go your way, carrying the things that you idolize, or does your God carry you? The idols of the modern English-speaking world are not images but more subtle things, such as money, pleasures, lusts; yet as life draws to its end they let you down. The God, whom we know, revealed in our Lord Jesus Christ, carries us through to the finish, for we are in the embrace of the love that will never let us go.

Hence, as verse 5 declares, God stands out alone, beyond all comparison with any other. This fact is supported by a further reference to the follies that are inherent in idolatry. Here are men falling down and worshipping a god, fashioned by their own hands, which is a stationary object, unable to move or speak or save. And here is the true God, who acts and speaks, and foretells things that presently come to pass. The "ravenous bird [bird of prey] from the east", is doubtless another allusion to Cyrus, whom He would raise up to execute His purpose in the near future. Then from that which was comparatively near the prophecy passes to the ultimate purpose of God, which was remote. At last God will place salvation "in Zion", which speaks of His intervention in mercy, and the redeemed Israel, who will enjoy it, will show forth the glory of the God who has accomplished it.

## CHAPTER 47

Chapter 46 commenced with a forecast of the Babylonian gods falling into ruin and captivity. Chapter 47 from start to finish pronounces judgment on Babylon itself. Just as the mystical Babylon of Revelation 17 and 18 is viewed as a woman, so here, only the picture is not so dark. Babylon here, for instance, is addressed as "virgin daughter", and not as "the great whore" and as "the mother of harlots". It is a solemn thought that the mystical Babylon, to which an apostate Christendom is working up, is more filthy in the eyes of God than the literal Babylon of Old Testament times.

The ancient Babylon was indeed for a short period "the lady [mistress] of kingdoms", but her downfall is foretold. Verse 6 strikes us as very remarkable, inasmuch as the things alleged against her had not actually taken place and did not come to pass till the days of Nebuchadnezzar. Then the wrath of God against the evils of His people condemned them to be carried away, and His inheritance polluted by the temple being destroyed. God permitted it; the Babylonian monarch did it with a heavy hand, and upon Babylon will come the heavy hand of God's judgment, in a day when there should be executed "the vengeance of the Lord our God, the vengeance of His temple" (Jeremiah 50:28).

So Isaiah was led to prophesy what Babylon would do to Jerusalem a century before it happened, and to foretell also how Babylon later should be overthrown, since Jehovah is "our Redeemer … the Holy One of Israel" (verse 4). He spoke too of the unexpected way in which the destruction would come upon them, as we see in verse 11, the fulfilment of which we find in Daniel 5.

Verse 13 speaks of the men who practised the dark arts of spiritism, in which Babylon trusted, for that city was apparently the original home of idolatry, which means the worship of demon powers. All such evil powers collapse when God acts in judgment. But it is this feature, we believe, that accounts for Babylon, rather than any other ancient city, being carried into Revelation with a spiritual application; for of that Babylon we read it had "become the habitation of devils, and the hold of every foul spirit", and again that by its "sorceries were all nations deceived" {Revelation 18:2, 23}.

## CHAPTER **48**

Having pronounced judgment against Babylon, the prophecy turns again in chapter 48 to the "house of Jacob, which are called by the name of Israel". The fact that they were thus addressed constituted a rebuke. Israel was the new name given to Jacob when God blessed him, as we learn in Genesis 32:28. The people claimed the new name, but were displaying all the ugly features of the old crafty, scheming Jacob. Outwardly they paid lip service to Jehovah and stayed themselves upon the holy city and the God of Israel, but without reality. They deceived themselves but not God, for He saw it was "not in truth, nor in righteousness."

This kind of thing has always been a great snare to the professed people of God. It came to a head, particularly in the Pharisees, when our Lord was on earth, and His most searching words of denunciation were directed against such. It is very prevalent today, for 2 Timothy 3:5 shows that "a form of godliness" may cover up hideous depravity. Let every reader of these lines, as well as the writer, beware of it. Spiritual pretension is a peculiar snare to those who are well instructed in the things of God, for they know the right and appropriate and even beautiful thing to say, and they may claim much without any heart and reality in it.

So the first eight verses of this chapter are filled with solemn words of exposure and warning. Here they were, trafficking with their idols, as verse 5 indicates, and giving them credit for anything favourable that came to pass, while still professedly serving God. And all the time it was God who was able to speak in advance and show the former things, and then suddenly bring them to pass, as verse 3 states. The fact was that their ears were closed to God's word so that they did not hear. They were marked by treachery and transgression as verse 8 declares.

Once more the obstinate sins of the people are thus exposed — so what then? Just when we might have expected further announcements of coming judgment, God states what He proposes to do for the sake of His own Name and praise. He will defer His anger and not cut them off entirely, though He is going to pass them through the furnace of affliction. He will consider not only their ultimate good as a nation but also His own glory and the honour of His own Name.

In verse 12 God Himself is still the Speaker. He presents Himself, saying, "I am He", or, "I am THE SAME", for it is really a name of God. He is not only "the FIRST" but also "the LAST". When we reach the book of Revelation, chapters 1:17 and 22:13, we find the Lord Jesus claiming these august designations for Himself; and indeed we may discern Him as the Speaker in the Old Testament passage before us, for it was His hand that "laid the foundation of the earth" and "spanned the heavens", as Hebrews 1:2 assures us. He who had so wrought in creation would not fail to work out His purpose and pleasure on Babylon and the Chaldeans, and in favour of His people.

We may discern the same Speaker in verse 16. There may have been a more immediate application of verses 14 and 15 to Cyrus, who was destined to overthrow Babylon and grant a respite to the Jews, but the full and lasting fulfilment is only found in Christ, who is the Sent One of the Lord Jehovah; and that, whether we read the end of the verse as in our Authorised Version, or that the Lord God "hath sent Me and His Spirit", as in other Versions. In John's Gospel particularly is the Lord Jesus presented as "the Sent One". In the Acts we have the sending of the

Spirit. We may call the closing words of verse 16 a preliminary intimation of the Trinity, though the real revelation of it awaited New Testament days.

The coming of Christ having thus been forecast, the "Holy One of Israel" is presented as Redeemer and the One who will ultimately teach and lead the people in the way that will be for their profit and blessing, though for the moment they were not hearkening to His Word. The blessing they were missing by their inattention and disobedience is strikingly pictured in verses 18 and 19. There would have been peace based on righteousness. What they missed then, in a more material way, is now being proclaimed in a spiritual way in the Gospel.

Yet, as verses 20 and 21 show, God will work in days to come for the redemption of Israel from their foes, and do for them again what once He did when under Moses He brought them through the wilderness and into the land.

But this does not mean that God is going to condone evil. Far from it. To reach the blessing Israel must be delivered from their sin, since there is no peace for the wicked, as verse 22 asserts. This verse marks the end of a distinct section — the first 9 chapters of the closing 27 chapters — in which the main offence alleged against the people is their persistent idolatry. Against that dark background the only bright light shining is the predicted advent of Christ.

## CHAPTER 49

So as we commence chapter 49, and so pass into the central section, we immediately hear His voice in the spirit of prophecy, calling upon us to listen to Him. In the Gospel of John He is introduced to us as "the Word", the One in whom the whole mind of God is expressed; and at the transfiguration the voice out of the cloud said, "Hear ye Him." So we are not surprised that prophetically He should say, "Listen … unto Me". What might surprise us, and might well surprise an attentive Jewish reader, is that He should address His call to the "isles", and to "peoples from afar", for the word, we understand, is in the plural, indicating the distant nations, and not the people of Israel. But so it was; and thus at the start of this new section it is intimated that what He has to say, and what He will accomplish, will be for the benefit of all men and not only for the people of Israel.

His words will cut like a sword and pierce like an arrow when He comes forth from the Divine quiver, for He shall appear as the true Servant of God and the true Israel; i.e., "Prince of God". As the earlier chapters have shown the national Israel had been called to serve God but had failed completely. This true Israel is declared to be called from the womb, made a "polished shaft" to fly unerringly as directed, and in Him, Jehovah says, "I will be glorified." We can now say, In whom He *has been* glorified, and in whom He *will yet be* glorified in a supreme and public way.

And then, in our chapter, comes verse 4. How often it has been the case in this fallen world that the servants of God have had to taste the bitterness of defeat and apparent failure. Indeed it seems to have been the rule rather than the exception. The supreme example of this is found in our Lord Himself. He came, as the Apostle Paul states, "A Minister of the circumcision for the truth of God, to confirm the promises made unto the fathers" (Romans 15:8); but, rejected by "the circumcision", His mission from that standpoint was marked by failure. He did indeed labour, but it was "in vain". His strength was put forth, but "for naught". Thus it was to all appearance, and according to the judgment of man.

"Yet", says the Messiah, "surely My judgment is with the Lord and My work with My God." His labour, His work, the exertion of His strength was not in vain, for God had entrusted to His Servant a task far deeper and wider and more wonderful than being just "a Minister of the circumcision", as we shall find intimated in our chapter, though we must travel into the New Testament to get a full view of its greatness.

Into that full light we today have been brought, so that with full hearts we can take up the little hymn that begins,

His be "the Victor's name",

and go on to sing,

By weakness and defeat,
He won the meed and crown;
Trod all our foes beneath His feet,
By being trodden down.

# Chapters 49:5 — 51:16

In this remarkable chapter we have something in the nature of a dialogue. Jehovah's word to the Messiah, whom He addressed as the true "Prince of God", we found in verse 3. The lament of the Messiah, having wooed Israel in vain, is found in verse 4, and it was historically verified, as we are told in Luke 13:34. From verse 5 onwards we get the response of Jehovah to this lament. The latter part of verse 5 is really a parenthesis, giving us Messiah's confidence, based upon what Jehovah is about to say. Israel may refuse and be obdurate, but in the eyes of Jehovah He will be GLORIOUS — and that being so, nothing of God's purpose will fail.

The answer of Jehovah begins in verse 6. We are prophetically advised that in the coming of the Lord Jesus wider and weightier purposes were involved than the gathering and blessing of Israel and Jacob. Light was to shine for all the nations, and salvation was to be made possible and available to the ends of the earth. Here is a prediction that — praise be to God! — is being verified today. He is the salvation. It cannot be disconnected from Him, as the Apostle Peter made so plain before the Jewish council — see Acts 4:12.

But if we can see the fulfilment of verse 6 today, we wait to see verse 7 fulfilled in a future day, which, we trust, is approaching. Jehovah is truly the Redeemer of Israel, though the One whom He sent is despised and abhorred in the servant's place. The hour draws near when, in the presence of this Servant, kings shall rise from their seats and princes shall do homage before Him. Men refused Him but God has chosen Him.

Again in verse 8 we have the voice of Jehovah. The humbled Servant whom men would not hear has been heard by Him, helped and lifted up. And this has come to pass in "an acceptable time", and in "a day of salvation". The significance of this may have been lost on Old Testament readers, but the Apostle Paul seized upon it in 2 Corinthians 6:2. The rejection of the Messiah, foretold in verse 7, would result in His death, and He would be "heard" and "helped" by resurrection from the dead, and this was to inaugurate the "acceptable time" and the "day of salvation".

Almost exactly nineteen centuries ago Paul reminded the Corinthian saints that they were living in that wonderful epoch: it was NOW. The epoch of grace and salvation still persists. It is still NOW. May we all be stirred to evangelize, remembering that it may not last much longer.

But in the latter part of verse 8, and onwards to the end of verse 13, the prophecy carries us into the age to come. The once-rejected Messiah is to be "a covenant of the people", for they will not enter into blessing on the basis of the covenant of law. He, and He only, will bring to pass the blessing on earth so glowingly described in these verses, so that the very heavens as well as the earth will break forth into jubilant song.

Verse 13 however, seems to indicate that an afflicted remnant of Israel is mainly, if not exclusively, in view here. Some will be prisoners, some hiding in dark places; coming over the mountains from distant spots in north and west, and even from "the land of Sinim", which some identify with China. At last the comfort, announced in the opening verse of chapter 40, will have reached "His people", and those who for so long had been "His afflicted" will find mercy. MERCY, notice; not merit, as is shown so conclusively at the end of Romans 11.

And it will be unexpected mercy, as the succeeding verses show. Zion, representing the godly seed who will receive the mercy, will be tempted to think in their extremity that they are forsaken and forgotten by their God: but they are not. Amongst mankind there is no stronger tie than maternal love. Yet under extreme pressure even that tie may break. The godly in Israel have a tie with Jehovah that will never break. While they are disowned nationally and set aside, God has wider purposes of blessing, reaching out to the remotest peoples. Yet He is marked by the utmost fidelity to all His promises, given to those who are the seed of Abraham in a spiritual as well as a material sense.

This will be the case in such abundant measure that in verse 18 Zion is told to lift up her eyes and see her children flocking to her side. In the days of her sinful desolation all her children were lost; now they appear in such numbers that the land cannot contain them, and the Gentiles — even their kings and queens — will do them honour, and that because of the glory and power of their God.

But when this great mercy reaches Israel their plight will be very great, as we may infer from verse 24, and the opening verses of Zechariah 14 confirm the inference. Just when they appear to be the helpless captives of their foes there will be a tremendous intervention of Jehovah for their deliverance. The New Testament makes it abundantly clear that the Jehovah, who according to Zechariah 14:3 will "go forth, and fight against those nations", is no other than our blessed Lord Jesus Christ; and by His hands "the captives of the mighty shall be taken away, and the prey of the terrible shall be delivered".

This will be a work of redemption by power but, as we know, it will find its righteous basis in the redemption by blood accomplished at His first coming. At the present time the Jew still rejects the righteous basis while hoping for national deliverance. It will be otherwise when their Redeemer does appear in power. He will then be manifested as the "Mighty One" of poor crooked "Jacob"; and not merely as the Mighty One of Israel.

## CHAPTER 50

This prophetic strain now ceases, for in verse 1 of chapter 50 we return to the existing state of the people, estranged from their God. This was not from God's side but from theirs. If He had issued a bill of divorcement against them, it would have been permanent and they would have been "cast away" (Romans 11:1), as to which Paul says, "God forbid." The fact was that they had sold themselves into disaster by their many transgressions.

And there was more than this, for the succeeding verses are a prophetic arraignment of the people as to their rejection of their Messiah at His first advent. When He came, there was, as verse 2 predicts, none among the leaders of the people to answer to His call. As the Gospels record He came announcing the kingdom is at hand. Had He no power to bring it in? Did the establishment of the kingdom fail because He had not the redeeming energy? Why, He moved in the seas and the heavens with the power of the Creator! Yet He was to take a lowly and subject place.

The word "learned" in verse 4 really means a disciple or one who is instructed, and our Lord took that humble and subject place when He came as the Servant of the will of God. He had indeed the opened ear, as was also predicted in Psalm 40, and He took that place that He might be man's true neighbour and speak the word in season to him that is weary. Morning by morning He heard the words He was to speak to others; hence His own statement to His disciples, "the words that I speak unto you I speak not of Myself" (John 14:10).

And having taken this lowly place of Servant, He had to face the scornful rejection of men. Smiting, shame and spitting were to be His portion though He came in such grace with blessing for men. Nothing however moved Him from the path of devotion to the will of God. His face was set as a flint in that direction, and therefore the power of God was with Him.

Moreover, as verses 8 and 9 intimated, the day will come when He shall be vindicated and His adversaries confounded and brought under judgment. So here again, as is so often in these prophecies, the two advents are brought together though many centuries come between them. Verses 5-7 have been fulfilled when He came in grace. Verses 8 and 9 will be fulfilled when He comes in judgment.

Then in the two verses that close the chapter we pass from prophetic utterances to words of counsel and warning. There were those that feared the Lord and yet they walked in comparative darkness. This was acknowledged by the Apostle Peter, when in his first epistle he reminded the converts from Judaism, to whom he wrote, that they had been called "out of *darkness* into His marvellous light" (2:9). But while they still dwelt in darkness, waiting for the light, they were to trust in the name of Jehovah — for so He had revealed Himself to them — and stay themselves upon His faithfulness. This they did, as the opening chapters of Luke's Gospel show. Jesus was "the Dayspring from on high ... to give *light* to them that sit in *darkness*" (1:78-79); and in chapter 2, we are given a glimpse of the godly souls who were obeying the instruction given in verse 10 of our chapter.

But there were many in those days that did not fear the Lord nor obey the voice of His Servant when He came in grace, and there are today a multitude who are of the same mind. They kindle a fire of their own to illuminate the darkness, and in the light of it and of its sparks they pursue their way. This is figurative language; but how graphic and striking it is!

In this twentieth century men have created a huge bonfire which is throwing sparks in all directions, and it appears that "science" is adding fuel to its flames at a rate that is becoming alarming. The sparks that are generated by human cleverness are flying everywhere. So let us not miss the application of these two verses to ourselves. If saints of old were to trust in their God while they waited for the light, should not we, who walk in the marvellous light of the Gospel, be filled with faith in the God so perfectly revealed in the Lord Jesus? Yet all around us are the multitudes charmed and intoxicated with the myriad bright sparks that spring from the fire of human inventions and cleverness, though some among them — those who know most and think more clearly — have many a twinge of fear as to the end of it all. Verse 11 indicates the end.

Mankind will lie down in sorrow under God's heavy judgment hand.

## CHAPTER 51

Chapter 51 opens with a call to the godly; for such are those that "follow after righteousness". The figure of a quarry is used to direct their thoughts to their origin as descended from Abraham, who had originally been called out, and in whom the promises had been deposited. When Isaiah wrote, the people had for centuries been under the law of Moses and they might easily assume that they would ultimately attain to blessing on a legal basis. But they will not. The blessing will only be theirs on the basis of the covenant with Abraham. It will be theirs not on the ground of their merit but of God's MERCY, as the end of Romans 11 so clearly states.

Therefore, remembering His covenant with Abraham, God will yet "comfort Zion", and bring about rich earthly blessing. At the present time the diligent work of returned Jews is producing in the land fertility where barrenness has prevailed for many centuries, but there are forebodings and distress and a voice of anxiety rather than of melody. At present it is but a national and purely human movement.

Verses 4 and 5 show what will come to pass when the movement proceeds from God and they are obedient to His law and ordering. Then His salvation based on righteousness will be manifested. There will be blessing, not only for those whom He acknowledges as "My people" and "My nation", but also for "the peoples"; — for the word at the end of verse 4 and the middle of verse 5 is in the plural. The distant isles will be brought under Divine rule in that day. The secret of it all is this: — "on Mine ARM shall they trust." That ARM was introduced to us in chapter 40:10, and is a designation of our Lord Jesus in the power and glory of His second advent.

Earlier in the verse "Mine arms" are mentioned; these we believe to be glorified saints, enjoying a heavenly portion, such as those to whom the Lord spoke the words recorded in Matthew 19:28. In that day the trust of men, who are blessed, will be centred in Jehovah's mighty ARM, but saints will act as His "arms", deputed by Him to "judge the peoples".

What a wonderful day that will be; for nothing either in heaven or on earth is stable, as verse 6 declares. Things physical and men themselves pass away but the salvation which God will bring to pass in righteousness will abide. We are called upon to hearken to God's word in verses 7 and 8; and we who "know righteousness" cannot but rejoice that only what is established in righteousness will remain and all else will be worm-eaten and destroyed. In the assurance of this no saint need fear the reproach and revilings of men.

These verses have unfolded before our minds a glorious and desirable prospect, only to be realized when the Lord Jesus comes again. Hence the call of verse 9: "Awake, awake, put on strength, O Arm of the Lord". In prophetic vision John saw Him so doing, in Revelation 19:11-16, when He will be displayed as King of kings and Lord of lords. The Lord Jesus has ever been the Executor of the purposes of God. He acted in the mighty scenes of creation. It was He who cut in pieces Rahab — a name meaning "Arrogance", given to Egypt in contempt — and dried up the sea, when God brought the people under Moses out of the land of their bondage. When He puts on strength and acts in the future day, there will be a far greater deliverance, and the ransomed of the Lord shall return to Zion with singing, and their joy will be everlasting and not transient and fleeting as all joyful deliverances have been hitherto in this sinful world. We today may call upon the Arm of the Lord to awake, only the language we use is, "Even so, Come, Lord Jesus."

In verse 12 and onwards another call to the godly is before us. Their tendency was, as our tendency today is, to have their eyes on man, and fear as all his evil tendencies and activities are observed. But men die and the One who comforts His people is the Maker of heavens and earth. When God acts, where will the fury of the oppressor be? These striking verses are intended to put heart into the saints of God in all ages. They have done so in the past and doubtless they are doing so today, especially where saints are confronted with "the fury of the oppressor", whether he be Communistic or Romish.

God is far above the actions and agitations of men. The nations are like the sea with its roaring waves but He divides them at His pleasure. In verse 16 the One who is the Arm of the Lord is addressed, for He is the One who speaks on God's behalf, the Divine word being in His mouth; just as He is the One who acts beneath the Divine hand, and the result of the speaking and the acting is given.

The result is going to be threefold, as this remarkable verse states. The first is that the heavens are going to be planted. The reference here is not to creation, for that was mentioned in verse 13, but, as we believe, to what God is doing today. The Lord Jesus Himself said, "Every plant, which My heavenly Father hath not planted, shall be rooted up" (Matthew 15:13); thus showing that to plant is a figurative expression for establishing in a place of blessing. By the Gospel today men are being called out from the nations for His name, and theirs is a "heavenly calling" (Hebrews 3:1). The coming age will display that the heavens have been planted by the grace of God in this age.

Secondly, the foundations of the earth will be well and truly laid. Again, this not the material creation, but laying the moral foundations in righteousness, for at present "all the foundations of the earth are out of course" (Psalm 82:5). Through the centuries men have striven in vain to establish a righteous order of things and the best of them have utterly failed. They could no more accomplish it than they could reach up to plant the heavens.

But there is a third thing that is to be brought to pass: Zion is to be formally acknowledged as God's special people. The prophet Hosea lived about the time of Isaiah, and it was through him that God said, "Ye are *not* My people and I will *not* be your God" (1:9). So up to this present moment they are disowned, though not set aside for ever. The day will come when they will be owned and blessed.

And these wonderful results will come to pass through the One who is presented to us in Isaiah as not only the lowly Servant but also the mighty Arm of Jehovah — our blessed Lord Jesus Christ. No wonder that the next words of the prophecy are the call, "Awake, awake". Jerusalem will awake presently: let us, who are called that we may be planted in the heavens, see to it that we are very much awake today — awake to our God; awake to His service. We are exhorted to this in Ephesians 5:14.

# Chapters 51:17 — 53:9

It is worthy of note that in the passage before us there are three calls to *hearken* and three to *awake*. Those called upon to hearken in the early part of the chapter — verses 1, 4, 7 — are those who "follow after righteousness ... that seek the Lord"; those acknowledged as "My people"; and those "that know righteousness ... in whose heart is My law". The emphasis clearly is on righteousness, for nothing that contravenes that is going to stand.

The first call to awake is addressed to the "Arm of the Lord" (verse 9), for all is dependent upon Him. When the hour strikes for Him to awake and put on strength, there will be witnessed the awakening of Jerusalem, as indicated in verse 17, and again in the first verse of Isaiah 52. The awakening that will come to pass will not be merely a political or national one, but will rather involve a deep spiritual work, as is made plain when chapter 52 is reached. It will come to pass only when Jerusalem shall have suffered to the full the chastising government of God, having drunk to the dregs the cup of *His* fury and of *their* trembling.

So first of all, in the closing verses of chapter 51, we get a recital of the effect of these disciplinary dealings, and then the declaration of how God will reverse the process, and chastise those who inflicted judgment upon Israel. But there will have been not only the sword of their enemies afflicting them but also famine, which comes from the hand of God. Under the affliction they are depicted as "drunken", but it is added, "not with wine". When the Arm of the Lord awakes on their behalf, the hour of their deliverance will strike, and the "cup of trembling" be taken out of their hands and put into the hands of their oppressors.

## CHAPTER 52

Then it is that Zion and Jerusalem not only will awake but also will put on strength, as the first verse of chapter 52 says. The language is figurative but quite clear in its import. At last holiness will mark the city and all that defiles be outside. It will be like a resurrection from the dust of death, and a release from the bands of captivity. They had sold themselves by their idolatry and sin, and gained nothing by it. Now they are to know redemption, but not by a money payment, as was customary in the days of slavery. The price of their redemption is unfolded when we come to chapter 53.

In verse 4, Egypt and Assyria are mentioned. In Daniel 11 these are referred to as "the king of the south" and "the king of the north", and at the present time these two powers are coming into prominence. They are noted by God, and from them Israel will be redeemed; but only when the prediction of verse 6 comes to pass.

When owned as "My people", they will have come really to know Jehovah. He will present Himself to them as "I am He … behold it is I." Darby's New Translation informs us that we have here the same expression as in chapter 41:4, and it might be translated "*I the Same.*" All their long centuries of sin and defection have not altered His nature and character in the slightest degree. What He was to them at the outset, that He is to them still.

They will discover too that the Messiah, whom they crucified, is "the SAME, yesterday, and today, and for ever"; and then the glorious tidings of verse 7 will be announced. To Zion it will be said, "Thy God reigneth", and in the light of the New Testament we well know the Person in the Godhead who will actually ascend the throne. Then at last there will be the *peace*, the *good*, the *salvation*, of which this verse speaks. The feet of him who shall herald such news will be beautiful indeed. As Christians we know these things already in a spiritual way, and the heavenly regions, rather than Jerusalem and its mountains, are our place. But though that is so, let us rejoice in the coming deliverance of Zion, and the beauty of the One who is going to accomplish it.

The verses that follow state the happy effects that will be seen when in the Person of the once rejected Messiah God is reigning in Zion. Watchmen usually lift up the voice to *warn* but now it will be to *sing*, and moreover there will be no disharmony for they will agree in what they see. And indeed the joyful song will be universal, breaking forth even in "waste places of Jerusalem". It will be a song based upon the redemption wrought for them by the Lord.

It is remarkable how throughout the Scriptures singing is recorded as the response to redemption. Though songs are mentioned as something that might have taken place, in Genesis 31:27, the first actual record of singing is in Exodus 15, when Israel had been redeemed out of Egypt. Then in Psalm 22, where the death of Christ for our redemption is prophesied, the first result mentioned is a *song*, though the word does not actually occur in the Psalm. It does occur however in Hebrews 2:12, where the Psalm is quoted. Again, just after the verses before us, we get the wonderful prophecy of the death of Christ in Isaiah 53; and the very first word of chapter 54 is, "*Sing*".

In verse 9 of chapter 51, the Arm of the Lord was called upon to awake: in verse 10 of our chapter it has awakened, and the mighty effect of the awakening has been unveiled in the eyes of all the nations. Not only Israel but all men will see the salvation of God come to pass.

Verses 11 and 12 stand by themselves and reveal another effect of this great work of God. Hitherto defilement had marked the people, whether personal or caused by lack of separation from defiling things. The double cry of "*Depart*", indicates urgency. Neither Israel nor we who are Christians are to traffic in unholy things. *Separation* is essential, for as Titus 2:14 tells us, Christ "gave Himself for us, that He might redeem us from all iniquity". This we have to learn, and Israel too will learn it in the coming day.

And if they or we should feel that to depart thus from iniquity is sure to cost us much, we need nevertheless have no fear about it. In our passage verse 12 gives Israel the needed assurance. God will be their Defender, and cover their rear as they depart from the evil. A similar assurance is given to us in 2 Corinthians 6:17-18, where God in His Almightiness and Majesty declares He will own as His sons and daughters the saints who are separate from the world and its evils.

With verse 13 there begins the central chapter of the last 27. As before pointed out, the 27 divide into three sections of 9 chapters; each section ending with solemn judgment upon the wicked — 48:22; 57:21; 66:24. In this central chapter of the central section we reach the *supreme height* of the prophecy, and are at once confronted with one of the greatest of the Divine paradoxes, since at the same time we touch the *deepest depths* into which the Messiah descended for our sakes.

In chapter 49 Jehovah's Servant was presented as apparently failing in His mission to Israel, and yet glorious in the eyes of God. Now His public exaltation and glory are declared, since He has acted with such great prudence, or *wisdom*; and in 1 Corinthians 1:23-24, we are told that "Christ crucified" is not only the power but also "the *wisdom* of God." His exaltation shall be definitely related to His previous humiliation. "As many were astonished" at the depth of His suffering and degradation; "SO ... the kings shall shut their mouths at Him", silent and ashamed. Some translate "astonish" instead of "sprinkle". If, however, the word "sprinkle" be retained, we should connect it with the use of that word in Ezekiel 36:25, where it clearly has the force of an act of blessing toward Israel.

The general force of these three verses that conclude our chapter 52 is perfectly clear. This meek and lowly Servant of Jehovah, who descended to such unheard of depths of humiliation, is going to come forth in a power and splendour that will astonish all mankind. His exaltation in the heights shall be commensurate with the depths into which He went. Now, *who believes that*?

## CHAPTER 53

This is exactly the question with which chapter 53 opens. This being the prophetic report; who believes it? And further; who recognizes that the suffering Servant and the glorious Arm of Jehovah are one and the same Person? We must underline in our minds the last word of verse 1, for we should never have discerned it had not a *revelation* been made. A parallel thought occurs in Matthew 16:17, where Peter's recognition and confession of Christ as "the Son of the living God", was declared by our Lord to be the fruit of *revelation* from the Father. That revelation — whether we express it as given in Isaiah or in Matthew — has come, we trust, to every one of our readers, and a thrilling revelation it is. The chapter proceeds to show that the rejection and death of the humbled Servant does not in any way contradict the predictions of His coming glory as the Arm of the Lord, but is rather the great foundation on which it is securely based.

Verse 2 presents Him to us in two ways. First, as He was in the eyes of God. Mankind in general, and Israel in particular, had proved themselves to be "dry ground", quite unproductive of anything that was good; yet out of this there sprang up this "tender plant", which drew its life and nourishment from elsewhere. The Lord Jesus truly sprang out of Israel, through the Virgin Mary His mother, but the excellence of His holy Manhood was due not to her but to the action of the Holy Spirit of God.

But second, He is presented as He was in the eyes of men. He had "no form nor lordliness" (New Trans.), nor the kind of beauty that men admire and desire. Some haughty, imperious man of imposing appearance would have caught the popular fancy; but instead of this He was "a Man of sorrows, and acquainted with grief", as verse 3 says. Being who He was, such a One as He could not be otherwise, as He entered and walked through a ruined creation with all its degradation and woe. This men did not understand, since they were insensible to their own degradation, and consequently they despised and rejected Him, as the prophet here predicts.

How do we Christians go through the world today? Let us challenge our hearts. The world today is in principle what it was then. Here and there more polish may be seen on the surface, but on the other hand the population of the earth has increased enormously, and so its miseries have multiplied. Hence, as the Apostle has told us, "the whole creation groaneth and travaileth in pain together until now" (Romans 8:22), and we who have the firstfruits of the Spirit are involved in it and groan within ourselves. Now groans are the expression of sorrow. He who today most largely enters into heaven's joys will most keenly feel earth's sorrows.

The language here is remarkable. The prophet is led to predict the rejection of Christ in words that will express the feelings of a godly remnant of Israel in the last days, when Zechariah 12:10-14 is fulfilled. Then they will say, "*we* hid as it were our faces from Him … *we* esteemed Him not." Identifying themselves with the sin of their forefathers, they will confess, not that the forefathers did it, but that *we* did it. This will be a genuine repentance.

Moreover their eyes will be opened to see the real meaning of His death, as verses 4 and 5 show. In the days of His flesh men observed His sorrows and His grief, and deduced from them that He was disapproved of God and therefore afflicted by Him. Now the real truth of it all bursts upon their hearts. They will discover what has been revealed to us, as recorded in the Gospel: He exerted His miraculous power with such sympathetic effect in the healing of men's bodies, "that it might be fulfilled which was spoken by Esaias the prophet, saying, Himself took our infirmities, and bare our sicknesses" (Matthew 8:17).

But if verse 4 is their confession of the truth concerning His wonderful *life* of sympathetic and sorrowful service, verse 5 gives the confession they will make as the true meaning of His *death* dawns upon them. They discover that He died as a Substitute, and it was even for themselves. This discovery we all make today as we believe the Gospel. The word *substitution* does not occur in this verse, but the truth that word expresses does occur four times in this one verse, and it occurs ten times in this one chapter.

Now here is a remarkable fact: — as printed in our English Bibles, verse 5 is the central verse of this chapter, which really begins with verse 13 of chapter 52. It is therefore the central verse of the central chapter of the central section of this latter part of Isaiah. And without a doubt it predicts truth which is absolutely central to our soul's salvation and in our soul's experience. The transgressions, the iniquities were *mine*, each of us has to say, but the wounding, the bruising were not mine but *His*. The peace, the healing are *mine*, but the chastisement, the stripes that procured them, were not mine but *His*. In all this He was my *Substitute*.

This thought is again emphasised in verse 6, and it is made plain that His substitutionary work was the fruit of an act of Jehovah, for He it was who laid our sins upon Him. In these verses, we must remember, the "we" and the "us" are those who believe, whether ourselves today or the godly remnant of Israel presently. And those who believe are those who have first confessed their sinnership; all going astray like lost sheep, though the way we took may have differed in each case. Sin is lawlessness; the doing of our own will, regardless of God's will, and the going of our own way independently of Him.

In verses 7-9, we have a series of remarkable prophecies, all of which were fulfilled on the very day of our Lord's death. Indeed it has rightly been pointed out that at least

24 Old Testament prophecies were fulfilled in the 24 hours that comprised that day of all days, when the Son of God bowed His head in death.

Verse 7 emphasises His silence before His accusers. When men are oppressed and afflicted unjustly, to protest is natural and most usual, so His silence was contrary to all experience, and it is noted in the Gospels — Matthew 27:11-14; Mark 15:3-4; Luke 23:9; John 19:9. Truly a sheep is dumb before the shearers, as anyone may observe today if they stand and watch the shearers at work, but He was not like a sheep being *sheared* but rather like a lamb led to the *slaughter*. He was indeed "the Lamb of God", as John the Baptist proclaimed, yet no word of protest escaped His lips.

Then further, "He was taken from prison [oppression] and from judgment", for it is still what men did to Him that is before us in these verses. If we turn to Acts 8:26-40, we find that the Ethiopian had in his reading of Isaiah reached exactly this point when Philip intercepted him in his chariot. He was doubtless reading from the Septuagint version in Greek, which renders it "in His humiliation His judgment was taken away". It was so indeed, for the trial of our Lord, resulting in His condemnation and crucifixion, was the most atrocious miscarriage of justice the world has ever seen. A legal expert has surveyed the evidence of the Gospels, and stated that every step taken by His accusers and judges, whether Jews or Gentiles, was irregular and unjust.

And the prophetic declaration of the result is "He was cut off out of the land of the living", or as the Ethiopian read it, "His life is taken from the earth". Hence the prophet says, "Who shall declare His generation?" and to this question men would unanimously reply that, His life being taken, no generation was possible. When we reach verse 10 of our chapter we shall find the answer which Jehovah gives to this question, and it is a very different one, inasmuch as He was cut off and stricken not for Himself but for the transgression of those whom Jehovah calls "My people". We have left the verses which give confessions which godly Israelites, and ourselves also, have to make, for oracular statements made by the prophet in the name of Jehovah.

So also in verse 9 we hear the voice of the Lord, declaring how He would overrule the circumstances connected with His burial: — "Men appointed His grave with the wicked, but He was with the rich in His death" (New Trans.). And so it came to pass. He was crucified between two wicked men, though one of them was gloriously saved before he died; and if men had had their way they would have flung His sacred body with those of the thieves in a common grave, but by the intervention of Joseph of Arimathea this was prevented, and His body lay in the new tomb belonging to Joseph. God always has the needed man for His work. Joseph was born into the world to fulfil that one line of Scripture! That one act covers all that we know of Joseph. In doing it He served the will of God.

In the margin of our reference Bibles we are told that in the Hebrew the word "death" is really in the plural — "DEATHS". It is what has been called the plural of majesty. Though crucified between two thieves, His death was MAJESTIC — ten thousand times ten thousand and thousands of thousands of deaths rolled into one.

By Joseph's act the prophecy of Psalm 16:10 was also fulfilled. The Holy One of God was not suffered to see corruption. He had done no violence nor was there deceit, or guile, in His mouth. Violence and corruption are the two great forms of evil in the earth. Both were totally absent in Him. Without corruption in His Person and life, there was no touch of it in His death or His burial. Thus far we have seen how God overruled the purposes of wicked men. In the remaining verses we are to see what God Himself achieved in His death and the mighty results that are to follow for Him and — blessed be God! — also for us, who believe in His name.

# Chapters 53:10 — 55:13

Thus far this great prophecy of the sufferings and death of the humbled Servant of the Lord has dealt with them mainly from the human and visible side: it now proceeds to deeper things, outside the range of human sight. Verses 10-12 predict what Jehovah Himself wrought, and what He will yet accomplish by means of it.

The holy Servant was to endure bruising and grief, and even have His very soul made an offering for sin: and all this at the hands of Jehovah. What it all really involved must ever lie beyond the reach of our creature-minds, even though they have been renewed by grace. And that "it pleased the Lord" to do this, may seem to us an astounding statement; yet the explanation lies in the latter part of the verse: since the results that should be achieved were to be of such surpassing worth and wonder. A parallel thought as regards the Lord Jesus Himself seems to lie in the words, "Who for the joy that was set before Him endured the cross" (Hebrews 12:2).

What are the results as stated in verse 10? They are threefold. First, "He shall see His seed". This carries our thoughts on to the Lord's own words recorded in John 12:24. Falling into the ground and dying, as the "corn of wheat", He brings forth "much fruit", which will be "after His kind", if we may borrow and use the phrase which occurs ten times in Genesis 1. This will be seen in its fulness in a coming day when: —

> God and the Lamb shall there
>   The light and temple be,
> And radiant hosts for ever share
>   The unveiled mystery.

Every one in those radiant hosts will be "His seed".

And in the second place, "He shall prolong His days", in spite of the fact that He was to be "cut off out of the land of the living", as verse 8 has told us. His resurrection is not stated in so many words, but it is clearly implied in this wonderful prophecy. In risen life His days are prolonged as the days of eternity. Raised from the dead, He "dieth no more: death hath no more dominion over Him" (Romans 6:9). In this risen life His seed are associated with Him.

And the third thing is that in this risen life "the pleasure of the Lord shall prosper in His hand." There have been devoted men who have served the Divine pleasure to a large extent, yet failing in many details. In the hands of the risen Servant all the pleasure of God will be fulfilled for ever. We have to pass into the New Testament to discover what that pleasure is, and how it will reach its culmination in the new heaven and new earth of which Revelation 21 speaks. The old creation on its earthly side was placed in the hands of Adam, only to be completely marred. The new creation will abide in untarnished splendour in the hands of the risen Christ. The light of this shines into our hearts even now; for as we sometimes sing:—

The new creation's stainless joy
Gleams through the present gloom.

Verse 11 gives us another great prediction. Not only is the
risen Servant to fulfil all the pleasure of Jehovah, but He
Himself is to be satisfied as He sees the full result established as the fruit of "the travail of His soul". We are little
creatures of small capacity, so that a very little will satisfy
us. His capacity is infinite; yet the fruit of His soul's travail will be so immeasurable as to satisfy Him. Do not our
hearts greatly rejoice that so it is to be.

The latter part of verse 11 in Darby's New Translation
reads, "By His knowledge shall My righteous Servant
instruct many in righteousness; and He shall bear their
iniquities." In these words "the many" are of course those
who by faith belong to Him: such receive the twofold
benefit — both the instruction and the expiation. Neither
can be dispensed with; and, thank God, both are ours in
this day of grace, as is so plainly stated in Titus 2:11-14.
Grace not only saves but also teaches us effectively to live
sober, righteous and godly lives. What is done for us today
will be done also for a godly remnant of Israel in the days
to come.

Now we reach the last verse of this great chapter. Note the
first word — "*Therefore*". Jehovah speaks, and declares
that because of what Jesus accomplished in the day of His
humiliation, He shall be assigned a great portion in the
day of glory. Now the whole passage began by the statement that "My Servant" is to be greatly exalted, and this
was followed by a challenge as to who believed that? — in
view of His humiliation and rejection and sufferings. This
last verse declares that instead of His sufferings being in
any way contradictory of His exaltation, they are the
secure basis on which His eternal fame and splendour will

rest. And further, what He has won is not for Himself alone, for He will divide the spoil with others who are designated "the strong". Our Lord's words, recorded in Matthew 11:12, may be an allusion to this, for strength was needed to receive Him, when the rejection of Himself and His claims was rising like a tidal wave to sweep all before it. Nor is the opposition of the world really otherwise for those who receive Christ in faith today.

The chapter closes with one more prediction as to the efficacy of His atoning sacrifice, coupled with one more detail that had to be fulfilled in His death. It was fulfilled when they crucified Him between two thieves, as Mark 15:27-28 records. It is remarkable how the *soul* of Christ in connection with His sacrifice is emphasised in this chapter, for we have the two statements — Jehovah made His soul an offering for sin, and also that He poured out His soul unto death. In Hebrews 10 the emphasis is placed upon His *body*, which was prepared for Him, and which He offered, as stated in verse 10 of that chapter. In each of the four Gospels His *spirit* comes into prominence. In John's Gospel the record is, "He delivered up His spirit" (New Trans.). No wonder then that the sins of the "many" — those who believe on Him — have been borne and for ever put away.

Closing the chapter, one asks oneself with wonder, How could Isaiah have written such words as these, some centuries before they were fulfilled in Christ, save by direct inspiration of the Spirit of God?

## CHAPTER 54

Chapter 54 proceeds to unfold the results for Israel of the sufferings of her Messiah, and the first word is "Sing". The marginal reading of Psalm 65:1 is "Praise is silent for Thee, O God, in Sion." Thus indeed it is today. But the time is coming when, as one of the fruits springing from Christ's sacrificial death, Israel — the true Israel of God — will break forth into singing. That people who were so barren and unfruitful under the law, when on that basis outwardly married to Jehovah, will be not only joyful but abundantly multiplied and blessed.

Graphic figures of speech are used to set this forth. Her tent is to be enlarged, her cords lengthened, her stakes strengthened. The holding strength of stakes depends much on the nature of the soil into which they are driven. When Israel drove her stakes into the law, they gave way almost at once. Driven into the grace of God, which will find its expression in the atoning death of their Messiah, they will be made strong for ever.

The One who will be their "Husband", will be their "Maker" as the Lord of hosts, and also their "Redeemer" as the Holy One of Israel, and He will be known as the God of *the whole earth*. The Gentile nations surrounding Israel were inclined to regard Him as Israel's own God, while they each had gods of their own; and even in Daniel, when Gentile nations were concerned, He is presented as "the God of *heaven*". In the millennial day He will be known as the God of the whole earth, though His centre will be in Israel.

How striking the contrasts which we find in verses 7-10. This time in which Israel is "Lo-ammi", covering more than two thousand years, may seem long to them, but it is "a *small* moment" to Him. When at last they are regathered it will be with "*great* mercies", dispensed righteously, since God's humbled Servant had borne their iniquities. Lay stress also on the word "*mercies*", for no thought of *merit* will enter into their blessing. This is fully corroborated in Romans 11:30-32.

Again, the Jew lies nationally under wrath. It lies upon them "to the uttermost", as Paul says in 1 Thessalonians 2:16. Yet, viewed in the light of the coming mercy, it is seen as "a *little* wrath", and the kindness that will be extended to them in mercy will be "*everlasting*". Hence "the waters of Noah" are cited; for as, when that judgment was over, God promised that such judgment should never happen again, so Israel will be beyond judgment for ever.

Verse 10 reveals the basis of this assurance. A "covenant of *My* peace" will have been established, based upon the fact that "the chastisement of *our* peace" (53:5) was borne in the death of their Messiah. This covenant of peace will no doubt be identical with the "New covenant", which Jeremiah prophesied in his 31st chapter. Its details are given there, but the righteous basis on which it will rest we have just seen, revealed through Isaiah. We may remember also the New Testament word, "The blood of the everlasting covenant" (Hebrews 13:20).

The closing verses of this chapter reveal something of the blessings that will be Israel's portion when the covenant is established. Verses 11 and 12 may speak of favours of a material sort, but verse 13 indicates spiritual blessing. All the true children of Israel will be taught of God — and His teaching is of an effectual sort — their peace being *great,* because it will be founded on righteousness as the next verse indicates.

Adversaries there will be, and they will gather together to disturb the peace, if that were possible. Of old God did use adversaries to chastise His people, but in the day now contemplated their gathering will be "not by Me", and it will only result in their own overthrow. When Israel stands in Divinely wrought righteousness neither weapon nor word shall prevail against them. It is remarkable how righteousness is emphasised here, wrought on their behalf by the suffering Servant of chapter 53. It reminds one of the way righteousness stands in the very forefront of Gospel testimony, as we see in Romans 1:17.

## CHAPTER 55

Chapter 55 opens with a call to "*everyone* that thirsteth", and so we pass beyond the confines of Israel to consider in prophetic outline blessings that will reach to the Gentiles through the work of the Servant who has died. Illustrations of this we see in Acts 8 and 10. The Ethiopian's thirst led him to take a long journey to Jerusalem, seeking after God: the thirst of Cornelius led him to prayer and almsgiving. In both cases, seeking for water to quench their thirst, they got *more*, even "wine and milk without money and without price." Moreover they got it by inclining their ear and coming to the Fountain-head. They heard and their souls lived; just as the prophet said in these verses. Thus we can see how strikingly his words forecast the Gospel which we know today. So even Gentiles are to enjoy the blessings of "the everlasting covenant".

Preaching in the synagogue at Antioch, the Apostle Paul cited the words "the sure mercies of David", and connected them with the resurrection of the Lord Jesus. These words connect themselves also with what we find in Psalm 89, particularly verses 19-29. In that Psalm *mercies* are specially emphasized, and the "David" is God's "Holy One" (verse 19), who is to be made "My Firstborn, higher than the kings of the earth" (verse 27), and "My covenant shall stand fast with Him" (verse 28). Clearly the Psalm contemplates the Son of David, of whom David was but the type. All the mercies of the Psalm will only be verified in Christ risen from the dead. Foremost in those wonderful mercies are the forgiveness of sins and justification from all things, which Paul preached at Antioch, and which were so well responded to by *Gentiles*, as Acts 13 records.

Gentiles are definitely in view also in verse 4, since the word "people", which occurs twice, should be in the plural. God's Holy Servant, risen from the dead, is given as "a Witness to the *peoples*, a Leader and Commander to the *peoples*." As the Witness He makes God known to men. As the Leader and Commander He brings men into subjection to God. This will be fully seen in the coming age, when "men shall be blessed in Him: all nations shall call Him blessed" (Psalm 72:17); but the same thing is realized in principle today as men from a thousand different peoples hear the Gospel and discover in Jesus the One who has been made both Lord and Christ. Let each reader challenge his or her heart. Have I fully received His witness? Is He indeed Leader and Commander in my life?

If verse 1 gives a *call* to all who thirst; and verse 2 presents an *argument*, intended to enforce the call; and verse 3, an *invitation* to life and mercy; verses 4 and 5 make very definite *announcements*. Only the announcement of verse 4 is addressed to men, whereas in verse 5 we find Jehovah's announcement to His Servant risen from the dead, stating in different words what had been said in verse 6 of chapter 49. This has definite application to the present age, when God is visiting the nations and taking out of them a people for His Name, and it is connected in our verse with His present *glory*. His people will be willing in the day of His *power*, as Psalm 110 predicts; but many from among the nations are running to Him in this day, and while He is glorified on high.

Verse 6 follows this by offering what we may call *a word of advice*, followed in verse 7 by *a word of assurance*. There is a time when God is near and may be found in grace, and a time when He retires from the scene to act in judgment. How often are these words uttered when the Gospel is preached, for the day of salvation is NOW. The assurance is that if any, however wicked they may be, turn to the Lord in repentance, there is mercy for him. The forsaking of one's thoughts and way is just what genuine repentance involves. Faith, we know, is needed too, but when Isaiah wrote, Christ the great Object of faith, though predicted, was not actually revealed. Consequently faith is not brought to the fore in the Old Testament as it is in the New.

But it is true at all times that the soul returning in repentance finds mercy, and the offer here is not only of mercy but of pardon in abundant measure. As the margin tells us the Hebrew is that He will "multiply to pardon." Such is the freeness and the fulness of the Divine mercy to the truly repentant.

Now all this is not according to the thoughts and the ways of men, as was well known to God. Hence what we have in verses 8 and 9. Indeed the whole of this magnificent prophecy concerning the death and resurrection of Christ, and the glorious results flowing therefrom, is totally opposed to human thoughts and ways. Christ, when He came, had nothing about Him that appealed to human thoughts and ways, as is stated in the opening verses of chapter 53, and what was true in Him personally is equally true of all God's ways and of His thoughts expressed in those ways.

But fallen man, alas! is self-centred, and prefers his own thoughts and ways to God's, ignorant of the awful gulf that lies between them, represented as the difference between the height of the heavens and of the earth. In

133

these days of giant telescopes, which reveal the unimaginable height of the heavens contrasted with our little earth, we can perhaps better realize the force of this. God's thoughts are revealed in His purposes, with which His ways are consistent, and now that they have come to light in connection with the Gospel, they form a lesson book for angels, as is shown in 1 Peter 1:12.

Moreover, besides the *thoughts* and *ways* of God there is His *word*, by which He signifies what His thoughts and ways are. Verse 10 assures us of its beneficent effect. Just as the rain descending from heaven brings with it life and fertility in nature, making man's labour to be fruitful for his good, so the word of God acts in a spiritual way. Received into the heart it is *fruitful* in life and blessing; and not only that, but is full of *power*, never failing in the effect that God intends whether in grace or in judgment. This was exemplified in the Lord Jesus Himself. No word of His ever fell fruitless to the ground, for He was the Living Word. It is equally true of the written word of God. It is said of the blessed man of Psalm 1 that "In His law doth He meditate day and night." Happy are we, now that we have "the word of His grace" (Acts 20:32) as well as the word of His law, if we do so likewise.

God's coming grace to Israel is in view here, as the two verses that close our chapter show. The peace that had been announced in the previous chapter should without fail be theirs, and joy also. Creation too will rejoice when the millennial day is reached. It is guaranteed here by the unfailing word of God, and when we turn to such a scripture as Romans 8, we are told how creation will be delivered from the bondage produced by the sin of man, and brought into the liberty of the glory of the sons of God, and we are carried beyond that which will be true for Israel into the largeness of the thoughts of God for the whole creation.

Thus all through the wonderful passage that has been before us we can note that what the prophets stated in germinal form comes into full revelation when, Christ having come and died and risen again and ascended to glory, the Holy Spirit was given to take of the things of Christ and show them unto us. May we have hearts that receive them and appreciate their unique value.

# Chapters 56:1 — 58:14

## CHAPTER 56

At the end of chapter 55 the wonderful prophetic strain, concerning the One who was to come forth as both the "Servant" and the "Arm" of the Lord, comes to an end. In chapter 56 the prophet had to revert to the state of things among the people to whom previously he addressed himself.

He spoke in the name of the Lord, and the fact that He called for equity and justice reveals that these excellent things were not being practised among the people. His salvation and righteousness were "near to come", though not fully revealed until after Christ came. When we open the Epistle to the Romans, we meet with both salvation and righteousness in verses 16 and 17 of the first chapter. Both are fully manifested in the death and resurrection of Christ; not as antagonistic the one to the other, but in the fullest agreement and harmony. While waiting for this manifestation the man who lived in accordance with righteousness would be blessed indeed. The sabbath was the sign of God's covenant with Israel, therefore it must be observed faithfully.

Moreover the blessings, that came from obedience to God's holy requirements in His law, were not confined to the seed of Israel, but extended to the stranger who sought the Lord. This passage, verses 3-8, is one to be noted with care. The door was open to any, no matter whence they came, who really feared the Lord and sought Him and His covenant amongst His people. The Queen of Sheba, for instance, came to question Solomon, not because of his vast knowledge of natural history, and his great literary output (see, 1 Kings 4:29-34), but "concerning *the name of the Lord*" (1 Kings 10:1). So too the eunuch is specially mentioned in our passage, and in Acts 8 we have the story of the Ethiopian eunuch, who was indeed one of the "sons of the stranger", who were seeking to "join themselves to the Lord, to serve Him, and to love the name of the Lord". What was promised to such by the prophet here was made good to him only in a more abundant measure, since he was not given a place "in My holy mountain", but rather "called … into the grace of Christ" (Galatians 1:6).

Even under the law the Divine thought was, "Mine house shall be called a house of prayer for all people." This is just the scripture quoted by the Lord on His last visit to the temple, just before He suffered; and He had with sorrow to add, "but ye have made it a den of thieves" (Matthew 21:13). Such was the awful state into which the Jews had lapsed, and we are painfully aware that they were well on the way to it as we read this book of Isaiah. Yet the gracious promise of verse 8 abides. God will yet gather a remnant of His people, who are outcasts amongst men, and when He does so He will gather others, who hitherto have been strangers. Today God is specially concentrating upon the strangers, visiting "the Gentiles, to take out of them a people for His name" (Acts 15:14).

Having uttered the promise of God, the prophet now turned abruptly to denounce the state of the people, and especially those who were in the place of watchmen and shepherds. The one were both blind and dumb, the other greedy for their gain and not for the welfare of the sheep. As a result the beasts of the field would break through and devour: a warning this of oppressing nations about to assail them from without, while those who should warn and defend were like drunkards, filled with false optimism.

## CHAPTER 57

Hence the opening words of Chapter 57. The time had come when God would remove from their midst the righteous and the merciful, and so it might appear as though these were under His judgment; whereas the fact was that it were better for them to be removed by death than to live to share the judgment that would fall. A striking example of this was seen somewhat later when God-fearing Josiah was taken away that his eyes might not see the disasters impending. It could then be said of him that "he shall enter into peace".

The evil state of things that existed among the people is again exposed, beginning with verse 3. Even in Hezekiah's day the state of things was thus. Reading the account of his reign in both Kings and Chronicles we might imagine that the mass of the nation followed their king in the fear of the Lord, but evidently they did not, and idolatrous evils still largely characterized the people. Down to the end of verse 14, these idolatrous practices and the moral filthiness that accompanied them are denounced, and it is plainly foretold that, even when disaster came upon them from without, no object of their veneration would be able to deliver them. Their works, and what they considered to be their "righteousness", would be of no profit to them. The whole spirit that animated them was wrong.

The right spirit is indicated in verse 15. Jehovah presents Himself in a light calculated to produce that right spirit in those that approach Him. He is high and elevated in the depths of space, far above this little world. He inhabits eternity, not restricted by the times and seasons that confine us. His name is "Holy". Are we sensible of this? If so, we shall at once be contrite as regards the past, and humble in the present. And it is the heart and spirit of the humble and contrite that God revives, so that they may dwell in His presence in the high and holy place.

These things were promised to those that feared the Lord in Israel in the past days, and they are more abundantly true for us today, who are not under the law but called into the grace of Christ. Self-satisfaction and pride are the last things that should characterize us. We may well rejoice that we know God as our Father; but let us never overlook the fact that our Father is *God*.

The succeeding verses go on to speak of God's governmental dealings with the people. He had to deal in wrath with them because of their sin and rebellion, but He would not contend with them as a nation for ever. The moment would come when He would heal and bless, and establish peace, both for those far off and for those near. The term "far off" may refer to the sons of Israel, who would be scattered, as distinguished from those who would be in the land. But what is said is true, if we understand it as referring to Gentiles, who were "far off", in the sense of Ephesians 2:13. But also in either case the peace has to be "created" by God, and is not something produced by men. Chapter 53 has told us how the peace is created.

The peace is only for those who are brought into right relations with God. It is not for the wicked who, far from Him, are as restless as the sea. The winds keep the sea in perpetual agitation. Satan, who is "the prince of power of the air", keeps the wicked in a condition similar to the sea, and all their visible actions are like "mire and dirt."

Hence there can be no peace for the wicked. This solemn statement closed the first section of nine chapters. There seems however to be a deeper emphasis in its repetition, since we have now had before us the judgment of sin in the death of the Messiah, the sinless Substitute, in chapter 53.

## CHAPTER 58

The third and last section of nine chapters now opens with a command that the prophet himself had to fulfil. Loudly and forcibly to accuse the house of Jacob of their transgressions and sins was no pleasing task; rather one that would be met with resentment and anger. The same thing however is necessary in connection with the Gospel today. In the Epistle to the Romans the Gospel is not expounded before the sinfulness of all mankind is plainly and fully exposed. In the Acts of the Apostles we see the same thing in practice. In Acts 7, Stephen did it with great power, and paid the penalty with his life. The same thing in its measure marked the public preachings of Peter and Paul; and when Paul faced Felix privately, "he reasoned of righteousness, temperance, and judgment to come", so much so that Felix trembled. We venture to think that this solemn note has far too often been missing in these days, as the Gospel is preached.

Verses 2 and 3 reveal why such a testimony of conviction was so needed, and for just the same reason is it needed today. The sins of the people were being covered up with a round of religious duties. They were going up to the temple, apparently seeking God. They took delight in acquaintance with God's ways, in observing His ordinances, in fasting and afflicting their souls. Were not all these outward things enough, and to be commended?

Yet they were but a mask, and when this was removed, what was beneath? Verses 3-5 show us what was beneath. Their "fast" was really a time of pleasure. There was exaction, strife, debate, the ill-treatment of others, though they bowed down their heads in a false humility and spread sackcloth and ashes beneath them. Their fast was just a matter of outward religious ceremony, and had nothing in it of that inward self-denial that it was supposed to indicate.

Is this the fast that God had chosen? is what verse 6 asks. And verse 7 proceeds to indicate the fast that would be acceptable unto God. Before Him what counts is what is moral rather than what is ceremonial. By Hosea God said, "I desired mercy and not sacrifice" (6:6); and the Lord quoted this twice (Matthew 9:13; 12:7). Thus we see here exposed the hypocrisy that came into full display and reached its climax in the Pharisees when our Lord was on earth; and as often noticed the severest denunciations that ever fell from the lips of our Lord were against the Pharisees. To none of the publicans and harlots did the Lord utter such words as are found in Matthew 23:1-33.

This evil was plainly visible in Isaiah's day; but having exposed it, the prophet was led to show that if his rebuke was accepted and the people repented there was yet blessing in store for them. Then, of course, they would walk in righteousness, and as a result there would be for them light and health and glory. The light would be like the dawning of new day. Their health would spring forth speedily. Their righteousness would open the way before them, and the glory of the Lord would protect their rear. Is Israel ever going to achieve this desirable state as the result of their law-keeping? The answer is, No. The New Testament makes this very plain.

Will this state then ever be reached? The answer is, only through their Messiah, whom they have rejected. When first He came, it was as "the Dayspring from on high" (Luke 1:78); it was the dawning of a new day in which Israel's light was to break forth. But they would have none of Him. What is predicted here is deferred consequently until He appears again in His glory. They will then be a born-again people, with the Spirit poured forth on them as objects of Divine mercy. Then, and not till then, will the glory of the Lord be a guard to their rear.

But in Isaiah's day the people were still being dealt with as men in the flesh and on the ground of their responsibility under the law, so the blessing proposed is based on their obedience. Hence there is found that fatal "If…" in verse 9. When the law was given it was "If ye will obey…" (Exodus 19:5), and so again is it here; and thus it must be as long as a law regime prevails. All through Israel's national history there has never been the taking away of the things mentioned in verse 9, nor the drawing out of their soul to the things mentioned in verse 10. Hence the good things of verses 11 and 12 have never yet in any full sense been realized, though a limited revival was granted under the leadership of Zerubbabel, Ezra and Nehemiah.

The fatal "If…" meets us again as we look at verse 13. This time it is linked with the due observance of the sabbath, and this seventh day was given to Israel, we must again recall, as the sign between themselves and God, when the law was given, as is stated in Ezekiel 20:12.

Sabbath-keeping had therefore a very special place in the law economy. If therefore the people turned away their foot from its due observance and merely used the day for the doing of their own pleasure, it was to do despite to the covenant of which it was the sign. This is just what the people were doing in the days of Isaiah.

In John 5 we read how the Lord Jesus healed the impotent man on a sabbath day. This gave great offence to the Jews and because of it they sought to slay Him. The Lord's answer was, "My Father worketh hitherto, and I work." The fact was that the covenant of law which demanded works of obedience from Israel, was hopelessly broken, and the sabbath, which was the sign of it, *was being set aside.* The time had now arrived for the work of the Son and of the Father to come into display, as indeed it did on the first day of the week, when our Lord rose from the dead, now known to us as "The Lord's day".

We can however read the last verse of this chapter, as also the verses that precede, as setting forth what God will eventually bring to pass for Israel in the millennial day that is coming, not as the result of their doings, but solely as the fruit of what their Messiah has already done, coupled with the righteous power to be put forth when He comes again in His glory. Then Israel will be like "a watered garden" and "the old waste places" shall be built. Then shall Israel delight itself in the Lord, and consequently "ride upon the high places of the earth".

They are far from doing this at present; but they shall certainly do so. And, Why? "For the mouth of the Lord hath spoken it." His word is stable. What He says always comes to pass.

# Chapters 59:1 — 60:5

## CHAPTER 59

The glorious promises contained in the closing verses of chapter 58 may have sounded idealistic and visionary even in Isaiah's day, and more so in our day, when in spite of every effort the problem of Israel and its land seems insoluble. What has delayed, and still delays, the realization of such promises? The opening verses of chapter 59 give the answer.

Unbelieving men would make Israel's plight a ground of complaint and reproach against God. Either He was *indifferent* so that His ear never caught their cries, or He was *impotent* and unable to deliver them. The true state of the case was that their sins had driven a wedge of separation between them and God. They were utterly alienated from Him.

This is a matter that some of us are inclined to overlook. In considering the havoc sin has wrought, we are apt to think mainly of the guilt of our sins and the judgment they will incur; perhaps also thinking of the enslaving power exerted by sin in our lives, while giving but little thought to the way in which it has separated us from God.

But none of the effects of sin is more disastrous than this — *alienation*.

If any desire proof of this, let them read Romans 3:10-12. The whole human race having fallen under the power of sin, there is none righteous; and, worse still, sin has darkened the understanding, so that by nature men do not realize the seriousness of their plight. Worst of all, sin has undermined and alienated their beings so that none seek after God. That being so God must seek after man, if ever he is to be blessed: in other words, God must take the initiative. We fall back therefore upon the sovereignty of God. To the recognition of His sovereignty God was leading the people through Isaiah, as we shall see before we reach the end of this chapter.

But before that is reached Isaiah has to speak to the people again in the plainest and most detailed fashion about their manifold sins. This is ever God's way. He never glosses over sin, but exposes it before men's eyes, that they may be brought to repentance. The preacher of the Gospel today had better recognize this fact. The deeper the work of repentance in the soul the more solid the conversion-work that follows.

Verses 3-8 give in full and terrible detail the sins that had separated them from their God, and we note that the indictments of verses 7 and 8 are quoted in Romans 3, in support of the sweeping statements of man's utter ruin, to which we have already referred. And further, having quoted these verses and others from the Old Testament, the Apostle Paul observes that these things were said "to them who are under the law"; that is, the denunciations are against not Gentiles but Jews, who were the picked sample of the human race. If true of them, true of all.

145

If in verses 3-8 the prophet speaks on God's behalf, denouncing the sins of the people, he turns in verses 9-15 to make confessions on behalf of the people, such as well might be made by those in their midst who feared God. He owns the miseries that existed on every hand: — no justice, obscurity and darkness just as if they had no eyes, desolation and mourning; every kind of oppression, false-hood and injustice rampant. Anything like truth utterly failing. A darker picture can hardly be imagined.

And one further feature of a very grievous sort was to be seen. There were some, however few they might be, who walked in the fear of God and hence departed from all these evils and walked in separation from them. Such came under judgment from the mass who went on with the evils; for "he that departeth from evil maketh himself a prey". It was a very unpopular thing to do, since it cast a discredit and rebuke on the mass who indulged in the sins. The same thing may be seen today, though the injunction to depart is far clearer and more definite: — "Let every one that nameth the name of Christ [or, the Lord] depart from iniquity" (2 Timothy 2:19). Such departing is no more popular today than it was then, but it is the clear command of the Lord to the saint of today.

Such being the state of things in the Israel of those days, and more or less so ever since those days, what will God do about it? The answer begins in verse 16. As we indicated a little earlier, God falls back upon His sovereignty in mercy. He indicates that though there was no hope in man, His mighty "Arm" would act and bring salvation. So here we have prophesied that which the Apostle expounds more fully in the closing verses of Romans 11. Through the Gospel at the present moment salvation is being brought to Gentiles in the mercy of God, but when "the fulness of the Gentiles be come in", God will revert to His promises to Israel, and they will be saved; but not as the fruit of law-keeping. It will be altogether as the fruit of His sovereign mercy. The contemplation of this wonderful mercy to Israel, as well as to us, moved the Apostle to the magnificent doxology with which he closed that chapter.

In the closing verses of our chapter the "Arm" of verse 16 is to be identified with the "Redeemer" of verse 20, and this verse is referred to in Romans 11:26, and the verbal differences we notice between the two passages are instructive. The Redeemer is now referred to as the Deliverer, for the Arm of the Lord will prove to be both. When He came as the humbled Servant of the Lord He accomplished redemption's mighty work. When He comes to Zion in His glory, He will bring the deliverance, made righteously possible by the redemption.

Then, according to Isaiah, He will come "unto them that turn from transgression in Jacob"; whereas in Romans we read that He "shall turn away ungodliness from Jacob". This again is what He will do in His delivering might, while Isaiah shows us rather how He will do it. He will come unto the God-fearing in Jacob, when judgment falls upon the evil-doers.

Verses 17 and 18 of our chapter speak of the judgment that must be executed by the Arm of the Lord. There is *"no man"* who can act and be an intercessor, just as earlier we saw that *"none* calleth for justice". No man has any merit, and no man is able to act to put things right. This latter fact we meet with again in very striking form in Revelation 5, where *"no man"* was found worthy to take the book of judgment and break its seals, save the Lamb that had been slain. What is so plainly shown in the Revelation is indicated in our verses. The Arm of the Lord

147

will be clothed in righteousness and salvation. The salvation will reach His people, but His righteousness will bring fury and recompence to His adversaries, so that from west to east the name of the Lord will be feared and His glory known.

But how does it come to pass, we may ask, that there will be found the God-fearing remnant in Jacob when this tremendous hour is reached? This is answered for us in verse 19. The testimony of Scripture is clear that just before the Redeemer comes to Zion, the enemy will have "come in like a flood". This will be the case in a double sense. According to Psalm 2, the kings of the earth and the rulers will have set themselves against the Lord and His Anointed, and Jerusalem will be the target for *antagonistic nations*; but also, Satan having been cast down to earth, as related in Revelation 12, *spiritual wickedness* will reach its climax. But just then, the enemy coming in like a flood, the Spirit of God will act to raise up a "standard", or "banner", against him.

The meaning of this is clear. Another scripture says, "Thou hast given a banner to them that fear Thee, that it may be displayed because of the truth" (Psalm 60:4). Just when the enemy's action reaches flood-tide height, there will be the counter-action of the Spirit of God, and true servants of God will be raised up, men who will "*turn from* transgression", and welcome the delivering might of the Arm of the Lord. Then at last the ungodliness of Jacob will be *turned away* for ever.

The permanence of this delivering work is stated in the last verse of the chapter, in which the Lord addresses the prophet as the representative of the nation. In that day they will possess two things: — "My Spirit" and "My words". When the sons of poor, failing Jacob shall be dominated by the Spirit of the Lord, so that they walk in obedience to the words of the Lord, their full blessing will have come.

And the same thing in principle stands true for us today, while we wait for the coming of our Lord. We have the Holy Spirit, not only "upon" us but actually indwelling us, and we have not merely certain words put in the prophet's mouth, but the completed word of the Lord, bringing us the full revelation of His purpose for us and of His mind and will for our earthly pathway. We may note also that through Haggai the prophet, God encouraged the remnant who had returned to Jerusalem under Zerubbabel in a similar way. In verse 5 of chapter 2 we have "*the word* that I covenanted with you", and "*My Spirit* remaineth among you: fear ye not." May similar encouragement be ours today. No matter what disastrous things have transpired in the history of Christendom, the Spirit of God and the word of God still remain.

## CHAPTER 60

Chapter 60 opens with a note of jubilation and triumph. The Redeemer having come to Zion, according to this prophetic strain, and God's covenant, connected with His Spirit and His words, being established, what else could we expect? Two things will then mark the people of Israel. They will "arise", since they have been sleeping in the dust of spiritual death among the nations. Further they will at last "shine" as a testimony for God, and their light be seen among the nations. This hitherto has never been the case. And, why not? Because the law of Moses, under which they have always lived, has only proved that they have no light *in themselves*. They will only shine when the light of God, concentrated as it is in their once-rejected Messiah, shines *through them*.

At His first advent Jesus came as the dawning of a new day, bringing light to those sitting in darkness, as we see in Luke 1:78-79. But the Jew rejected the light and as far as they were concerned they put it out. Consequently, as we saw in chapter 49, He was given for "a light to the Gentiles" to be "My salvation unto the end of the earth." His second advent will be in "the day of Thy power" when "Thy people shall be willing", according to Psalm 110. Then at last they will come into the full blaze of that light and reflect it, as the moon reflects the light of the sun.

This thought, that of reflected light, is clearly in the verses that open chapter 60. The earth will be filled with darkness of a very gross sort at the time when Christ comes again. This He Himself indicated when He said, "Nevertheless when the Son of Man cometh, shall He find faith on the earth?" (Luke 18:8). It will be rare and but little in evidence. During His absence there is no light save that connected with faith. When He comes, the glory of the Lord will be manifested, and it will be seen upon Israel, and so reflected on them and in them that the Gentiles shall come to the light that shines through them, and "kings to the brightness of thy rising."

Again we have to say that in principle this applies to us who are of the church while we wait for Him. To Christians of Jewish extraction it is said that they had been brought out of darkness "into His marvellous light" (1 Peter 2:9); and to those who were brought in from among the Gentiles it was said, "ye were sometimes darkness, but now are ye light in the Lord" (Ephesians 5:8). To them the word was added, "walk as children of light"; that is, their light was to shine out as a testimony to all around. Spiritual light is to shine forth from the saints of today, who form the church, while we wait for the shining forth of the glory in a fashion that all can see.

In an earlier chapter we have read what God's purpose as to the people of Israel was: "This people have I formed for Myself: they shall show forth My praise" (43:21). They have never yet done so in any proper sense, but in this coming day they will, and therefore they will become a centre of attraction upon earth. First of all the attraction will be felt by those who are truly of the Israel of God. Those who can be called "thy sons" will come to Zion from afar, and those who are "thy daughters shall be nursed at thy side." This will be a regathering of the true Israel in the land of God's choice that will altogether eclipse the migration of Jews to Palestine that we see still proceeding today. God will be behind the movement and the revelation of His glory in the once-rejected Servant, but now the mighty delivering Arm, will be the attractive force.

The effect of the revelation of the glory upon redeemed Israel is further shown in verse 5. True, it will not be essentially a matter of faith as it is with us today, for, says the prophet, "then thou shalt *see*". The thing will be manifest before every eye, and the result will be threefold. They will "flow together"; so the drift will be in the direction of *unity*, and the old divisions that have marred the nation will disappear. Then they will *fear*, and experience how true it is that "the fear of the Lord is the beginning of wisdom" (Proverbs 9:10). As a result of this they will "*be enlarged*".

We venture to think that this enlargement will take place not only in material things but also in mind and heart. It will take place in a material way, as the rest of verse 5 indicates, but the enlargement is clearly stated to be of the heart. The verse mentions the "abundance of the sea"; and frequently that figure is used to indicate the masses of mankind. The statement does not mean that Israel will be well supplied with fish, but rather that though evil men, far away from God, are like the troubled sea that cannot rest, in the coming age the spared nations will be like a placid sea, yielding its abundant treasures and converting them more especially toward Israel. This is further emphasized by the words that close the verse, which according to the marginal reading would be "the wealth of the Gentiles shall come unto thee."

And all this blessing, both material and spiritual, will be poured upon Israel when the Arm of the Lord is revealed in power and glory, and those who "turn from transgression in Jacob", that is, the true Israel, born again and in the presence of their Redeemer, stand in the virtue of His work. That work He wrought when He was despised and rejected of their forefathers and being led as a lamb to the slaughter, He was wounded for their transgressions and bruised for their iniquities.

As Christians we are today blessed with "all spiritual blessings", and that "in heavenly places in Christ". When Israel is blessed in this way on earth, we shall be in the fulness of blessing in heaven.

# Chapters 60:6 — 62:3

The abundance of things, in the form of earthly blessings, that will be poured into Israel, is given in much detail from verse 6 of chapter 60. In that verse Sheba is mentioned, the land from which came the Queen, who visited Solomon with much gold and spices. When she arrived, as related in 1 Kings 10, she showed forth the praises of Solomon. In the day contemplated in our chapter, "they shall shew forth the praises of the Lord."

This will come to pass in the way that is intimated in verse 7. Not only will the altar of God be once more established, but the house of the Lord be in their midst. A century or two after Isaiah, the prophet Haggai predicted that "the glory of this latter house" (2:9), or, "the latter glory of this house" (New Trans.), should be greater than the former in the days of Solomon; and so it will be. It is designated here as "the house of my glory", and even as such the Lord Himself will glorify it. In the glorified house of His glory His praises will be seen and heard.

We pass from the house to the people in verses 8 and 9. Today the Jews are returning to their ancestral home in their hundreds and thousands without faith in Christ. When God regathers His people it will be a quick and effectual work. They will "fly" — a speedy work. It will be "to their windows" — like a bird returning to its home. And this they will do as "doves" — a bird noted for its meek and quiet spirit. The unconverted Jew of today may still be just as Paul described his own nation in 1 Thessalonians 2:15, but the born-again Israelites, who will fly to their millennial home in the coming day, will be a repentant and meek people. The ships too of Gentile nations will carry them and their riches, acknowledging the name of Jehovah as "the Holy One of Israel". Inasmuch as He has been glorified, He can now glorify Israel.

In result, the nations, instead of being antagonistic, will be the helpers of their fame and prosperity, as we see in verses 10-12. As things stand today, nothing would seem more unlikely than what is here predicted; but we must remember that not only will there be a work of God in Israel, but among the nations also. In Revelation 7 we have not only a vision of the "sealed" among the tribes of Israel, but of a great company of the elect, drawn out of all nations; and in Revelation 21 we read of "the nations of them which are saved". Those who rebel among the nations will perish.

In result, Jerusalem will be acknowledged as "The city of the Lord, The Zion of the Holy One of Israel." It will have become what God intended it to be — "an eternal excellency" and "a joy". But again the basis on which this will be accomplished is made very plain. All will see that it is not something produced by Israel but rather by the One who is their Saviour and Redeemer. Jacob, the schemer, and his posterity have nothing in which to boast. The *Mighty One* of Jacob alone has done it on the basis of redemption.

We read of the Redeemer coming to Zion in verse 20 of the previous chapter, and noticed how the Apostle referred to this in Romans 11. We now see that the Redeemer is Jehovah. And in the New Testament it is equally clear that the Redeemer is Jesus. He who is the Arm of Jehovah IS Jehovah.

In our chapter this is stated in verse 16, and it is the fact that explains what otherwise would be a mystery; namely, the wealth and the glory that will be poured into and upon Israel from the Gentile nations, as we see detailed in the verses that precede and that follow. We read that "the nation and kingdom that will not serve thee shall perish". Why should such severe judgment fall? Because the Divine plan for the coming millennial age is that Israel shall be the central nation, surrounding His glorious temple, as a nation of priests, and that the other nations should be grouped around them, and expressing through them their submission and devotion to the King of kings. Should a nation in that day defy the Divine plan, they will perish. It will be the age of Divine *government*. We live at present in the age of *grace*.

In the latter part of Revelation 21 we have described the new and heavenly Jerusalem, which is "the Lamb's wife" — a symbolic description of the church in its heavenly position during the millennial age, and if we compare with it the details of our chapter concerning the earthly Jerusalem, we notice certain similarities, and yet striking contrasts. The presence of the Lord is the glory of both cities. The gates of both are open continually to receive the wealth and honour of the nations. Both have an abundance of "gold" and find their everlasting "light" in the Lord.

But the contrasts are more numerous. The gates of the earthly will not be shut day or night: of the heavenly not shut by day — but the day is an eternal one, for there is *no night* there. The glory of the earthly will be the temple, described in verse 13 as "the place of My feet". Jehovah will have His *feet* on the earth; but in the heavenly there is *no temple*, for "the Lord God Almighty and the Lamb are the temple of it." It is the place of His *presence* rather than the place of His feet. The earthly will know a glory brighter than the sun; but the heavenly will have no need of the sun for "the Lamb is the light thereof." Gold will be brought plentifully into the earthly; but in the heavenly it forms the street, and they walk on it. We think we may say that the difference is accounted for by the introduction, in Revelation, of THE LAMB.

But we can indeed rejoice in the description given us by Isaiah of millennial blessedness and glory, when righteousness and peace will mark the scene and violence will have disappeared; when the real walls of Jerusalem shall be salvation, and out of its gates shall issue praise. This will only come to pass when, as verse 21 says, "Thy people also shall be all righteous". That will only come to pass when the new birth, of which Ezekiel 36 speaks, takes place. Then God will "sprinkle clean water" upon them, and give them "a new heart", and put within them "a new spirit". Then, "born of water and of the Spirit", as the Lord Jesus put it to Nicodemus, they will see and enter into the kingdom of God.

When the children of Israel are thus born again and righteous before their God, through the grace of their Redeemer, they will be multiplied as the last verse of our chapter tells us. At last God is able to make of them "a strong nation". When the time arrives God will do it *speedily*. It will not be a long drawn-out process, a kind of evolution, such as men love, but a swift action, of a sort that manifestly is a work of God.

## CHAPTER 61

This attractive description of millennial blessedness is continued in chapter 61, but before it is resumed, the first three verses, forming a paragraph by themselves, instruct us further how all will be brought to pass. Here we have the passage that our Lord found in the synagogue at Nazareth, as recorded in Luke 4, and which He read, stopping in the middle of verse 2 because there the prediction of His first advent ends. The fact is, of course, that for Israel, as for us, everything depends on His two advents.

The words that were read by our Lord all indicate grace, without any allusion to the law of Moses. There is a veiled allusion to the three Persons of the Godhead. In our Bibles GOD is printed thus in capitals because it is really the great name, Jehovah. So the opening words mention the Spirit of Jehovah, the Lord Jehovah Himself, and the "Me", who is the Anointed One, or the Christ, who is sent to be the Proclaimer and the Minister of the grace. It is perfectly clear from Exodus 19 that the words of the law were not "glad tidings". There was "the voice of the trumpet exceeding loud; so that all the people that was in the camp trembled." The tragedy was that when a voice of exceeding grace was heard in the synagogue at Nazareth the people neither trembled nor rejoiced, but rose up with anger to kill the One who proclaimed "the acceptable year of the Lord."

Hence the necessity of those words which our Lord did not read. The second advent of Christ in power and glory, and in judgment, is foreseen to be a necessity by the prophet here. The glorious state of things predicted will never be established till Christ comes again. He laid the foundations for it in the redemption accomplished at His first advent. He will bring it to pass in power, and with vengeance, at His second advent.

Vengeance is truly a terrible word when it comes from the mouth of God, and if we turn to verse 4 of chapter 63 we shall find it referred to again. It means retribution exacted for wrongs committed, and all the wrongs that men have committed are primarily against God. A day is coming when God Himself will bring retribution on the heads of sinful men; judging "the world in righteousness by that Man whom He hath ordained", as Paul told the Athenians, recorded in Acts 17. When that comes to pass, it will "comfort all that mourn", because their mourning will be not for their own personal troubles, but rather for the evil and chaos that will fill the earth, the sinfulness of men having then reached its climax. When men have filled the cup of their iniquity to the brim, God will strike by the advent of Christ. And to those who mourn, though few in number, what a comfort that will be!

Verse 3 shows us what comfort it will bring such. Their previous state is described by the words "ashes", "mourning", "the spirit of heaviness". All will be changed for them. They will have "beauty", "the oil of joy", and "the garment of praise". They will be planted as "trees of righteousness", the trees of lawlessness and evil having been cut down, and in all this, and in them, the Lord will be glorified.

From verse 4 the description of Israel's blessings is resumed. Not only will the land be renovated, the desolate cities be built up afresh, and strangers who formerly despised them be their servants, but the crown of all be their spiritual blessing. They will be the "Priests of

Jehovah" and "Ministers of God" in the coming age, and as under the law the priests were supported by the offerings of the common people, so it will be for them, and that in abundant measure, for they are going to "eat the riches of the Gentiles". In that day even the Gentiles will have abundance, and out of their riches will flow abundance to the priestly nation.

This is indeed a remarkable prophecy as to the end God is going to reach in His dealings with His earthly people. Verse 7 speaks of shame and confusion, and these things have been their portion under the strong hand of their God in holy government because of their manifold sins, but now all is to be reversed. Other passages have shown us how their whole condition spiritually will have been reversed under "the everlasting covenant", of which verse 8 speaks. Based on the everlasting covenant will be the everlasting joy, predicted in verse 7. All will have to acknowledge that now, as a born-again people, they are "the seed which the Lord hath blessed."

In the two verses that close this chapter the prophet himself speaks, as voicing the glad response that will spring from the redeemed and restored Israel of the millennial day. At last Jehovah their God will be known and gloried in with joyfulness. At Sinai and under the law their ancestors feared and trembled before Him, since all depended on what they could do. Now they are joyfully alive to what God has done for them and with them. Notice how at this point the prophetic strain drops down to the personal and individual. It is not "clothed *us*", but "clothed *me*". Not "covered *us*", but "covered *me*". The language is figurative, but the meaning is clear. The individual Israelite of that glad day will be clothed with salvation, as the fruit of standing before his God in a robe of righteousness.

Though there is so wide a difference between the character of Israel's earthly blessing and that of the church's
heavenly portion, the basis on which both rest is evidently
the same. For them salvation is to be founded on righteousness, and so it is for us today, as is made so plain in
Romans 1:16-17. The Gospel is the power of God unto
salvation because in it the righteousness of God is
revealed, not acting against us but on our behalf by the
sacrificial death and resurrection of the Lord Jesus. It is
revealed "on the principle of faith to faith" (New Trans.).
It is brought to us, not on the principle of *works* which we
have to perform, but of *faith* as opposed to works. And it
is revealed, not to our *sight*, but to *faith*, where faith exists.

The believer today stands before God in righteousness
divinely wrought, and his faith apprehends this, though
there may be nothing of an outward sort visible to sight,
save the new kind of life he lives as the fruit of his conversion. But in this connection too there is contrast, for
outward and visible things will be clearly manifested, as
the robe of righteousness and garments of salvation
envelop the sons and daughters of Israel in that day. There
will not only be the transformation in the land and cities,
mentioned in verse 4, but the righteousness will blossom
forth in a way that will be visible to the eyes of all the
nations to the praise of the Lord, who has brought it to
pass.

So whether it be for the saint of today, called by the
Gospel to a heavenly portion, or whether for the renewed
Israelites of the future — salvation stands securely based
upon righteousness. And because righteousness will be
established, praise also will "spring forth before all the
nations." It will be so obviously the work of God that the
glory of it and the praise will be His.

## CHAPTER 62

In the first verse of chapter 62 we have the prophet speaking in the name of the Lord; or, perhaps we might say, it was the Spirit of Christ which was in him, speaking through him, in keeping with what we read in 1 Peter 1:11. If the result of God's work in Israel, and on behalf of Zion and Jerusalem, will bring such good to them and such praises to God, then there must be no rest until all is accomplished. Before the eyes of all the nations Israel will stand in a righteous salvation, which God Himself has wrought, and hence they will display His glory, and not their own. The figures used in verse 3 are very expressive of this. Previously, how different the situation! The Apostle Paul had to write concerning them, "The name of God is blasphemed among the Gentiles through you" (Romans 2:24). Now they will be "a crown of glory" and "a royal diadem" in God's hand.

We, who today are called for a portion not only spiritual but also heavenly, may well rejoice as we contemplate what God will yet do for and with His earthly people; and at the same time we may yet more rejoice as we think of what is purposed for us. If we scan the first two chapters of Ephesians, what remarkable expressions we find. The blessing purposed for us will be "to the praise of the glory of His grace", inasmuch as it is bestowed "according to the riches of His grace". And further we discover that "in the ages to come" God is going to display "the exceeding [or, *surpassing*] riches of His grace in His kindness toward us through Christ Jesus."

When Israel is blessed, as Isaiah foretells, it will be a work of grace and bring much glory to God. But when the church shines forth in the heavenly glory of Christ, her Head, there will be a yet brighter display of grace. Those embraced in the church have been gathered out of the nations through the centuries; not a few of them human beings of the most degraded type.

Holy angels have witnessed the whole tragedy of human sin. When a saint, that they recognize was once a vicious, savage cannibal, is shining in the glory of Christ, what will they say? They will surely confess that here is a display of SURPASSING grace.

And we, the saints of today, have the privilege of taking our part in God's present work by the Gospel. Do we realize this? If we do, we shall not fail to take our place, under the Lord's direction — whether to go, or to give, to speak or to pray — while waiting for the glorious consummation.

# Chapters 62:4 — 64:3

If verse 3 of our chapter predicts how the Israel of God in the coming age will be a crown of glory and a diadem in the hand of God, verse 4 declares the place of blessing that shall be theirs, in contrast with all that has characterized them hitherto. Several times already in reading this prophet we have seen that both they and their land have been forsaken by God because of their sins. To this day no interposition of God on their behalf, comparable to what He did when He delivered them from Egypt under Moses, has taken place. The delivering act of God is yet to come.

When it does take place by the appearing of Christ, it will be a repentant and born-again people who are delivered. As such they will be called "Married". The figure used in verse 5, that of a young man marrying a virgin people and their land, may remind us of the striking words of Psalm 110, where the people who refused Jesus in the day of His poverty will be willing in the day of His power, and the youth of Israel will rally to Him as the dew falls in the summer morning. Only then will Jehovah their God rejoice over them.

But though that is so, the forsaken Jerusalem is not forgotten by the Lord. This is expressed by the setting of watchmen on the walls, who are never to hold their peace until deliverance comes. It is worthy of note that Ezekiel was the prophet set as "a watchman unto the house of Israel" (Ezekiel 3:17), and he it was who in vision saw the glory of the Lord depart from the temple and the city. During Israel's night the watchmen are not to hold their peace. They are, so to speak, continually to be reminding the Lord that His glory is involved in the establishment of Israel in their land and Jerusalem becoming a praise to His name in the earth.

When we lift our thoughts from the earth and Israel's predicted place of blessing therein to God's purpose for the heavens and for the church, we may surely speak in similar fashion. When in response to our Lord's assurance of His advent we cry, "Even so, come, Lord Jesus", we are thinking, we trust, not only of the fulness of our own blessing in the heavens, but of God achieving in the church all He purposed before the foundation of the world. There will be "the redemption of the purchased possession, *unto the praise of His glory*" (Ephesians 1:14). As on the earth, so in the heavens, His glory will shine forth.

Yet after all the watchmen on the walls of Jerusalem are needed to keep God's purpose before the minds of men, rather than before the mind of God, since He never fails. God Himself has sworn that He will do it, and He swears by Himself, as Hebrews 6:13 reminds us. He connects His oath in verse 8 with "His right hand and by the Arm of His strength". So here again the Arm of the Lord is introduced, since it is by Him that the thing will be done; and the Arm is characterized by strength, for Christ is the power of God, as well as the wisdom of God, as we are told in 1 Corinthians 1:24.

Corn and wine are frequently mentioned together in Scripture as indicating the sustenance that man needs, both solid and liquid, only here we see that all will not only be secured to Israel but that it shall be enjoyed by them in the presence of their God; as it is put here "in the courts of My holiness."

The three verses which close the chapter give us a prophetic forecast of how this will be accomplished. In Isaiah, "the daughter of Zion" is an expression that occurs a number of times. The first occurrence is in verse 8 of chapter 1, and it seems to be identified with the "very small remnant" mentioned in verse 9. We believe that is the force of it here. The God-fearing remnant will be found scattered to the ends of the world. They will be called and a standard lifted up to which they will gather; and then their way to the holy city and through its gates will be opened up before them, and every stone of stumbling will be removed.

And how will all this be accomplished? By the advent of their Salvation, who is evidently a Person, in the light of the words that follow. By His reward and His work the Arm of the Lord will prove Himself to be God's "Salvation unto the end of the earth" (49:6).

And what will be the result as regards those who are gathered as "the daughter of Zion"? They will at last be exactly what Israel was originally intended to be — "The holy people"; that is, a people separated to God, in accord with His mind and nature. This delightful condition will only be reached since they will be "the redeemed of the Lord".

This redemption will be a vital and spiritual reality, and not just a national thing, without regard to the spiritual state of individuals, as when they were brought out of Egypt under Moses. It will be brought about by the grace of our God, and not on the ground of law-keeping. This is indicated very clearly in Romans 11, where Paul states that though at present shut up in unbelief, they will ultimately "obtain mercy." The coming salvation of the godly in Israel will be as wholly an act of Divine mercy as is the salvation of degraded Gentile sinners today. The mercy of God will reach both the people and their city.

## CHAPTER 63

But there is another side to this matter, which confronts us as we begin to read chapter 63. Israel's redemption will involve drastic judgment falling on all those who are foes of them and of God, just as judgment fell on the Egyptians, when Israel was typically redeemed in the bygone age. And He, who is to become Israel's Redeemer in power, is the One who will overthrow them. In verse 1 of our chapter, however, Edom is specially singled out as the one on whom the judgment is to fall. Now Edom is Esau.

In the Proverbs we read that, "A brother offended is harder to be won than a strong city" (18:19), and this has been exemplified in the history of Esau and Jacob. The feud today is as strong as ever. It underlies the situation of great danger that surrounds Palestine today. It will be decisively settled at the second coming of Christ. Some excuse might possibly be found for Edom objecting to the reoccupation of the land by unconverted Jews, but evidently their objection will be just as strong against any regathering of a converted people. He who will regather Israel will destroy them.

The figure of treading "the winepress" is employed in verse 3, and the same figure is used in the closing verses of Revelation 14. It evidently indicates judgment of a wholesale and unsparing kind. There is also of course judgment which discriminates between the righteous and the wicked, but then the figure of a harvest is used, as we see in Matthew 13:40-43, as it also is in earlier verses of Revelation 14, showing that judgment of both kinds will be executed in the coming day.

The whole of Obadiah's short prophecy is directed against Esau, and he makes it plain that just when "upon mount Zion shall be deliverance, and there shall be holiness; and the house of Jacob shall possess their possessions", the house of Esau "shall be for stubble", which gives us the same thought of unsparing judgment under a different figure.

In our chapter this judgment is presented as the personal act of the One who is called "Mine own Arm", taking place when salvation was accomplished on behalf of God and His people. At that solemn moment "the day of vengeance" will be in His heart, that day spoken of in chapter 61 verse 2, which our Saviour did not read in the synagogue at Nazareth. That *day* of vengeance will introduce the *year* of redemption for God's people. Judgment being God's "strange work" (28:21), it will be a "short work" (Romans 9:28). Hence vengeance is only for a day compared with the year of redemption. All this, be it noted, has to do with the government of God on the earth, and not with saints who today are being called out for a heavenly portion. As far as we are concerned Edom is just one of the peoples amongst whom the Gospel is to be preached, though, alas! so few from amongst them respond to it.

Having predicted the coming day of vengeance, the mind of the prophet turned back in verse 7 to contemplate the extraordinary goodness of the Lord in His dealings with Israel from ancient days. It had been a story of loving kindness and of mercies according to His own heart. He had adopted them as His people, accredited them with truthfulness and saved them from their oppressors. Moreover He entered into their afflictions, granted His presence, redeemed them from Egypt and carried and cared for them till they reached the land of promise. In Exodus 33 we read how God promised His *presence* to Moses and the people, and in the last chapter of that book it is recorded how the glory of the Lord filled the tabernacle. Also we read of the Angel of the Lord who went before them, who here is called "the Angel of His *presence*". In Malachi 3:1 the expression "Messenger of the covenant" is really "Angel of the covenant", and is clearly a prediction of the coming of the Lord Jesus; so here also we may see a reference to Him.

On God's part therefore nothing had been lacking in His dealings with Israel; so what had been their response to all this goodness? Verse 10 gives the sad answer, "But they rebelled, and grieved His holy Spirit". As a result of this His holy government had to come into action, and He became their adversary. Here we have in few words what Stephen amplified and brought up to date, as recorded in Acts 7. Here the prophet has to record that they *vexed* God's holy Spirit. Many centuries after Stephen says to them, "Ye do always *resist* the Holy Ghost". To grieve Him is serious indeed, but to resist Him is fatal.

As Isaiah saw it in his day, what was God's answer to this vexing? God remembered His original doings with Moses, and therefore there was hope in the prophet's heart, and still a basis on which he could appeal to the Lord. Again, in verse 12, the Arm of the Lord is discerned as He who acted at the Red Sea, and the people recognized that God had triumphed gloriously. Hence, on this the last time that the "Arm" is mentioned by Isaiah, the adjective "*glorious*" is attached to His name. Glorious He is indeed.

Verses 12-14 therefore summarize the kindly dealings of God with His people, when He brought them out of Egypt, led them through the wilderness, and finally brought them into the land. There was the acting of "His glorious Arm", and consequently He made for Himself "a glorious name" as well as "an everlasting name". Nevertheless Israel was still under the law, and hence the hand of God lay heavily on them in judgment.

Isaiah was conscious however that he could appeal to God on another ground than the law. So, having mentioned Moses in verse 11, in the closing verses of the chapter he makes a further appeal to God on the ground of their connection with Abraham, with whom was made the original covenant of promise. If we read Genesis 15, we see that the covenant embraced not only Abraham personally but his seed also, that was to include a great multitude. This covenant put his descendants through Isaac into a place of special relationship before God, and had no conditions attached to it.

Now Abraham, though "the friend of God", was but a man and had long since departed, and so was ignorant of them. Israel too — the name given by God to Jacob — might not acknowledge them. Yet Jehovah, who had included them in His covenant, was the abiding One, and from the outset He had been as a Father to them, for in another prophet we have Him saying, "I am a Father to Israel" (Jeremiah 31:9). Hence the appeal to Him here on that basis.

Two things strike us as remarkable here. First, in verse 17 the hardness of heart manifested in the people is traced back to an act of God. "Why hast *Thou made us* to err...?" Was this justified? Clearly it was, for just that was the original message given to Isaiah, in verses 9 and 10 of chapter 6. What had happened to them was in principle the same as had happened to Pharaoh. Long before, they had been warned, "Harden not your heart as ... in the wilderness" (Psalm 95:8), but to this no response had been given, and the time came in God's holy government when He sealed home this hardness of heart upon them; and as the result we have Isaiah's cry to God, Thou hast "hardened our heart to Thy fear".

Has such an action on the part of God any application to us today? Evidently it has, or we should not have found the warnings of Hebrews 3 and 4, based upon those words we have quoted from Psalm 95. In that Epistle, Jewish believers are taken up on the ground of their profession, and warned by the example of the Jewish people. Not all who *profess* the faith *possess* the vital thing. Hence the warning, "Take heed, brethren, lest there be in any of you an evil heart of unbelief".

There is also the terrible working of the government of God predicted for the end of our Gospel age, when as to those who refused the truth, "God shall send them strong delusion, that they should believe a lie" (2 Thessalonians 2:11). This most drastic action of the government of God will well befit the most drastic refusal of His truth that the world will ever witness.

In the second place it is remarkable how the prophet complains, in verse 18, not only of the brief occupation of the land of promise but also of the treading down of the sanctuary by the adversary. At the time of Isaiah's prophecy, as recorded in the opening of the book, this had not actually taken place, though there had previously been defeats, as in the days of Rehoboam. It appears that Isaiah was given to see the end to which the people were drifting, and to appeal to God in the light of it. That the sanctuary should be defaced by the adversary was the crowning blow. If that was lost, all was lost. In the light of this we can understand the touching appeal that is made, beginning and ending with what is called "the habitation of Thy holiness and of Thy glory".

## CHAPTER 64

Now what will have to take place if this appeal of the prophet is to be answered? Evidently that which he yearned for, as expressed in the first verse of the next chapter. God Himself must intervene in a very personal way. He must rend the heavens and come down. Nothing short of this would suffice. Yes, but how should this be done?

The words that follow make very plain what Isaiah had in his mind. He desired that God would personally intervene in power and in judgment. He knew that God had come down at the start of their national history, when there were thunders, lightnings, fire, and "the whole mount quaked greatly", even if it did not actually flow down at His presence. Now, if there were another such display of the Divine presence, surely the effect would be great.

It was, of course, something of this kind, that would break up the Roman power and work a visible deliverance for Israel, that the people, even the godly ones, connected with the coming of their Messiah; as we see so plainly manifested by the disciples, both before Jesus died and even after His resurrection. Something of that sort will take place at the second coming of Christ, as Zechariah 14:4 testifies. And for that coming we wait.

But we today are in the happy position of knowing that this desire for the presence of God has been answered first in another way. Earlier, Isaiah had foretold the coming of the One whose name should be Immanuel, and in the opening of Matthew's Gospel we are told the meaning of that name — *God with us*. The heavens were rent upon Him just as He came forth in public service. He came amongst us "full of grace and truth"; not doing "terrible things", but rather suffering Himself the terrible things, when He died as the Sacrifice for sin.

Compared with these prophetic desires, and even forecasts, into what "marvellous light" we have been brought!

# Chapters 64:4 — 65:12

It is striking how verse 4 follows what we have dwelt upon in the first three verses. Isaiah desired a mighty display of the power of God, such as had been manifested at the outset of Israel's history: yet he was conscious that God had in reserve things beyond all human knowledge, and prepared for those who waited for Him to act.

To this verse the Apostle Paul referred in 1 Corinthians 2:9, showing that though in ordinary matters men arrive at knowledge by the hearing of the ear — *tradition* — or by the eye — *observation* — or by what we may call *intuition*, these things can only reach us by *revelation* from God by His Spirit. Isaiah knew that there were things to be revealed. Paul tells us that they have been revealed, so that we may know them.

In keeping with this, the Apostle Peter has told us in his first Epistle that when the Spirit of Christ testified through the prophets, they "inquired and searched diligently" concerning what they had written, and they discovered that they were predicting things only to be made known to such as ourselves who are brought into the light of what Christ has accomplished. So again we have to remind ourselves how great are the privileges that are ours. God has indeed "come down", but in grace and not, for the time being, in judgment.

The prophet foresaw that when the prepared things were made known they would only be received if a certain moral state were found. There must be not only the waiting for Him but also a rejoicing in righteousness and working the same, as well as a remembrance of God in all His ways. Thus the godly remnant of Israel are described here. It will be so in a future day, and so it is today, since it is only by the Spirit that we perceive and receive the wonderful things now revealed. When, having been received, the Spirit of God is in control, we enter into the enjoyment of the things that God has prepared for those who love Him.

Now at that moment the necessary state did not exist amongst the people, hence we have the words, "Behold, Thou art wroth; for we have sinned". This confession is placed in brackets in Darby's New Translation, so that the following words spring out of the beginning of the verse. In *righteousness* and *remembrance* is to be "continuance, and we shall be saved." Isaiah had previously presented to us "a *just* God and a Saviour" (45:21); thus the people whom He saves must be brought into conformity with Himself.

Verses 6 and 7 continue the confession of sin that was interjected in verse 5. Notice the four figures that are used to express their sorrowful state. First, unclean, as a leper is unclean, in the sight of the law. Second, their "righteousnesses", that is, their many doings which they considered to be acts of righteousness, were but "filthy rags" in the sight of God. Third, as a consequence of this, they were all fading, dying things, like autumn leaves. Fourth, their sins were like a wind that blew them all away.

Are things different today? Has the spread of a civilisation based upon Christian ideals altered things? It has not, and things are just the same. The leprosy of sin is just as virulent; the outward righteousnesses of mankind are just as spurious; death is just as busy; the wind of God's judgment on sin will soon sweep all away.

Further, the prophet had to complain that no one was rightly moved by this state of things so as to call upon the name of God; no one was found to take hold of God in supplication and prayer. The fact was that God had hid His face from them in His holy government. It was a sad state of affairs when no one was stirred to take the place of an intercessor.

And without a doubt we may say the same as we look on the state of Christendom today. Bright spots there are, thank God! — spots where the Spirit of God is manifestly at work. But in spite of this, the picture over-all is a dark one. Evil abounds under the profession of Christ's name, and even where the Spirit of God is working, wholehearted servants of God are all too few. Who stirs himself up to take hold on God as to it? Who prays to the Lord of the harvest, that He will send forth labourers into His harvest? — as the Lord Himself directed in Matthew 9:38. May God Himself stir us up, instead of hiding His face from us, if we fail to stir ourselves up in this matter.

Now, in our chapter, comes the touching appeal to Jehovah. The very first words of Isaiah's prophecy were, "The Lord hath spoken, I have nourished and brought up children, and they have rebelled against Me." Very well then, Jehovah had taken the place of Father to Israel, and upon that the faith of the prophet counted, and on it he based his appeal. Moreover Jehovah was not only Father to them but He was as a Potter also. Israel was but the clay in His hand.

That this was so, and that God acknowledged it to be so, was made manifest a little later in the days of Jeremiah. In chapter 18 we read how he was instructed to go down to the potter's house and receive a lesson there. He saw the clay vessel "marred in the hand of the potter: so he made it again another vessel, as seemed good to the potter to make it." The Lord proceeded to tell Israel that they were in His hand as clay is in the hand of the potter, so He could do with them as seemed good in His sight. Confining our thoughts to Israel, we know that God will make another vessel, which is what the Lord Jesus was showing Nicodemus, as narrated in John 3. That which is born of the flesh — even Abrahamic flesh — is flesh. Only that which is born of the Spirit is spirit. Only a born-again Israel will enter the Kingdom.

In Isaiah's day the point as to "another vessel", made known to Jeremiah, had hardly been reached; hence here we have further pleadings with God on behalf of the marred vessel as we see in the four verses that close the chapter. "We are all Thy people", says the prophet, though about that time, or very soon after, Hosea's son had to be called "Lo-ammi: for ye are not My people, and I will not be your God" (1:9). These closing verses of appeal seem like a last cry to God, before the sentence of repudiation was given to Hosea.

The iniquity marking the people is confessed, but mercy is sought. The desolations mentioned in verses 10 and 11 strike us as being stated prophetically, for though the king of Assyria ravaged the cities of Judah in the days of Hezekiah, he was not allowed to take Jerusalem nor burn the temple. Jeremiah it was who actually saw these things fulfilled. Even in Hezekiah's day however, it was certain that these terrible desolations would come to pass, as we saw when reading the end of chapter 39 of this book. When they were accomplished Israel was set aside for the time being, and the times of the Gentiles began.

## CHAPTER 65

The two verses that commence chapter 65 are in exact harmony with this. They are quoted by the Apostle Paul in Romans 10:20-21, after he had shown that even Moses had upbraided the people and predicted that God would turn from them to others. Then he prefaced his quotation from our chapter by saying that, "Esaias is very bold...".

Yes, Isaiah does speak with great boldness, for he speaks as the very voice of Jehovah rather than speaking about Him. He does not say, "He is sought... He is found... He said..." but rather, "I am sought... I am found... I said...". How comes it, we may enquire, that people who never asked after God should be seeking Him? The answer seems obvious. It must take place as the result of God seeking after them. This is exactly what has taken place in this Gospel age. Israel being set aside, God goes out in sovereign mercy to Gentiles, as Paul goes on to explain in Romans 11. Has the wonder of this mercy penetrated our hearts in any substantial measure?

God's dealings with Israel, in setting them aside for this long period, is justified by what we read in verse 2. The people had been rebellious, following "their own thoughts", instead of God's thoughts as expressed in His holy law, and these thoughts of theirs led their feet into a way that was not good. God had condescended to entreat them "all the day", and that "day" had been a long one, extending over centuries of time. To these entreaties they had not responded.

The following verses lay specific evils to their charge, but before we consider them let us pause a moment to consider whether we have been guilty of pursuing our own thoughts instead of God's in that which has been revealed to us. His mind for us as individual Christians, and also as members of the body of Christ — the church — is plainly stated in the Epistles of the New Testament. Now it is sadly easy to slip away from these and walk after our own thoughts; and more particularly so in regard to church matters; easy to say, "That was doubtless right enough for the first-century Christians, but hardly practicable for us today." But it is God's thoughts and ways that are perfect, whilst our own thoughts lead us into "a way that was not good".

The evil ways of Israel were largely connected with idolatrous practices, as verses 3-7 show. The opening words of Deuteronomy 12 are, "These are the statutes and judgments, which ye shall observe to do in the land", and there follow prohibitions against the high places and groves, or gardens, and altars which the heathen nations had made. So God's way for them was that they should bring all their offerings to His place in Jerusalem; offering as He had commanded. But they preferred to worship according to their own thoughts with the result that is described in these verses. Their sacrifices were wrong; their altars were wrong; the food they ate was wrong; and to crown all this they affected a sanctimonious piety, which led them to say to others, "Stand by thyself, come not near to me; for I am holier than thou."

This plainly indicates that the evil of Pharisaism began early in Israel's history. The spirit of it is plainly visible when we read the prophecy of Malachi. It reached its fullest and worst expression in the time of our Lord, furnishing the main element which led to His crucifixion.

We may remember how He charged them with "Teaching for doctrines the commandments of men" (Matthew 15:9). So this quite agrees with what we have just seen stated by Isaiah. They preferred to walk after their own thoughts, rather than by the word of God. The same evil principle has persisted through the years, and it is all too evident today within the circle of Christian profession. Though their positions, both doctrinally and ecclesiastically, may widely differ, there are found those who demand separation — "Stand by thyself, come not near to me;" — based on a claim of superior sanctity or spirituality as the case may be. Such separatists are as offensive to God as "smoke in My nose, a fire that burneth all the day."

Now this state of things in Israel demanded a recompence of judgment from the hand of God. It would seem that this spurious sanctity on top of their rebellious disobedience was their crowning sin. It brought upon them the seventy years of captivity in Babylon; and, when those years had passed and a remnant came back to the land, the same hypocrisy sprang up in their midst again, rendered worse, if anything, by the very mercy that had been shown to them. They crucified their Messiah saying, "His blood be on us, and on our children." Thus it has been through their long centuries of trouble, and will yet be in the far worse sorrows of the great tribulation.

The lesson for us is that God desires obedience to His thoughts, expressed in His word. If that be our aim, we shall soon realize how little we apprehend them, and even more feebly carry them out, and this will produce in us a spirit of humility — the complete opposite to that of a spurious sanctity such as is revealed here.

Another note is struck when we reach verse 8. Under the figure of sparing a cluster of grapes, because it is of value for wine producing, God declares that He will spare a remnant of the people, though judgment must fall on the mass. This He will do, "that I may not destroy them all." This remnant is spoken of as "My servants", and in the next verse as "a seed out of Jacob", and also as "Mine elect", who will inherit the land.

We may remember how our Lord Himself was predicted as "Seed" of the woman, in Genesis 3, and again as the "Seed" of Abraham, concerning which the Apostle wrote, "He saith not, And to seeds, as of many; but as of one, And to thy Seed, which is Christ" (Galatians 3:16). When considering Isaiah 53, we also saw that the risen Christ is to "see His seed", as the fruit of the travail of His soul; and the same thought meets us at the close of the other great prediction of the sufferings of Christ in atonement — "A seed shall serve Him" (Psalm 22:30). He, who is pre-eminently the "*Seed*", is to have a *seed* of His own order in His risen life. This thought underlies the verses we are considering.

Two further things may be pointed out before we leave these verses. First, it was to this godly seed that the Lord Jesus referred at the beginning of His well-known "Sermon on the Mount". The prophet speaks of "an *inheritor* of My mountains", and says, "Mine elect shall *inherit* it". The third beatitude is, "Blessed are the meek: for they shall *inherit* the earth" (Matthew 5:5). Now this enlarges the promise, so that it applies beyond the confines of Jacob and Judah. It is the meek of all peoples who will inherit the earth, when Heaven's kingdom is at last universally established.

The second thing we have to remember is that this remnant according to the election of grace, called out from
the mass of the Jews, exists today, though by the very fact
of its calling it is severed from Judaism and its earthly
hopes. That it exists is made plain by the Apostle Paul in
the opening verses of Romans 11, and he cites his own
case as the proof of it. We have to read Ephesians 2, particularly the latter part of it, to learn the new position of
heavenly favour and blessing into which they are brought
in association with those called from among the Gentiles
by the Gospel that is being preached today.

In our chapter earthly blessing is before us, as verse 10
makes very plain. The valley of Achor was a place of judgment, as narrated in Joshua 7:24-26. That place of
judgment is to become "a door of hope", according to
Hosea 2:15. Our verse reveals it as a place of rest for flocks
and for men. Is there not a parable in this? Where judgment has been executed, there hope is to be found, and
rest is the final result.

We leave this beautiful picture when we read verses 11
and 12. God cannot forget the existing state of departure
and sin that marked the people in Isaiah's day. They had
forsaken Jehovah; they had forsaken His holy mountain,
whereon stood His temple. And to what had they turned?
The rest of the verse reveals it, though the translation is
rather obscure. In Darby's New Translation we find "Gad"
substituted for "that troop", and "Meni" for "that number", with footnotes giving an explanation to the effect
that the former word indicates "Fortune, or the planet
Jupiter", and the latter word "Number, or Fate, or the
planet Venus".

The people had turned aside to worship the heavenly
bodies, and connected their false worship with the

ISAIAH

gambling instincts which are so strong in fallen humanity.
If things went well it was Fortune. If badly, it was Fate. In
the minds of the people these were deities to whom they
made offerings of food and drink. As so often "table" is a
figure indicating solid food, as on the table of shewbread,
and wine furnished the drink. This throws some light on
the Apostle's words in 1 Corinthians 10:21, where he
mentions "the cup of devils" and "the table of devils". The
devils of this verse were of course demons; and demon
power lay behind the "Gad" and the "Meni" mentioned
here.

When, in verse 12, God says He will "number" them to
the sword, there is an allusion to the name "Meni", which
means number. The people are plainly told that judgment
and death lay before them. They were rejecting the law of
God. We are living in an age when men are rejecting the
grace of God; and to do this is more serious than to reject
law, as we are told in Hebrews 10:29. When the Gospel is
preached, let this be made very plain.

# Chapters 65:13 — 66:24

Though God has to pronounce judgment upon the evil-doers, which must be executed in due time, He delights in the mercy and blessing that He bestows upon His true servants. This He makes manifest in the passage which begins with verse 13. We notice, of course, that earthly blessings and earthly judgments are in view; food, drink, rejoicing and song on the one hand; hunger, thirst, shame and sorrow on the other. A curse and death will come upon them; their very name being considered a curse, while the chosen servants will be called by another name.

This will be fulfilled in days to come, but it is remarkable how we can see a fulfilment of it even in our day, which is explained by what the Apostle Paul wrote in 1 Thessalonians 2:14-16. On the other hand a remnant, according to the election of grace, is still being called out of that people and incorporated with elect Gentiles as the church of God. Upon such another Name is called, for they are CHRISTian.

As far back as chapter 42, we had Jehovah's declaration, "New things do I declare" (verse 9), and now we discover the wide scope of that declaration. There is to be a complete sweeping away of the old order and the creation of new heavens as well as a new earth. The verses that follow show that the millennial age is referred to and not the eternal state, which is announced in Revelation 21:1.

At present the heavens are the seat of Satan's power, as Ephesians 6:12 indicates. They will be in a new condition when those evil powers are cast out, and heavenly saints are installed, as from the New Testament we know they will be. When the Messiah acts as "the Arm of the Lord", and His dominion extends to the ends of the earth, it will be a new earth indeed. In comparison therewith the old order will be so horrible that men will banish it from their minds.

The remaining verses of the chapter give a description of the happy conditions that will characterise the millennial age, beginning with the joy and blessing of Jerusalem, which will be then, as always intended, the centre of earthly blessing. Yet it will not be an age of absolute perfection, as verse 20 shows. For the righteous, life will be greatly prolonged, yet it will be possible for sinners to be discovered and come under a curse. Still those who are the elect will have their days as the days of a tree, and we know how many a tree does not grow old for centuries.

Hence earthly blessings will be enjoyed to the full; houses, vineyards, fruit, and above all they will be in close touch with Jehovah their God. So much so, that not only will He hear them while they are yet speaking to Him, but He will answer their desires even before they express them by calling upon Him. This indicates that a place of remarkable nearness to Him will be theirs.

Moreover mercy will be extended even to the animal creation, which at the outset was placed under man, and so has suffered as the result of his fall. No longer shall strong animals slay and devour the weak. Those most opposed, like the wolf and the lamb, will feed together, and the most voracious, like the lion, will be satisfied with vegetable food. All hurt and destruction shall cease.

To this there will be just one exception. The serpent was used by Satan in deceiving Eve, and the curse upon it ran, "Upon thy belly shalt thou go, and dust shalt thou eat all the days of thy life" (Genesis 3:14). Now this sentence is not to be revoked. It seems that in the ranks of the lower creation it will be retained as a sign and reminder of the tragic effects of sin. The serpent will not be able to hurt nor destroy, but its degraded and miserable state will remain.

## CHAPTER 66

Chapter 66 opens on a very lofty note. The earth is but the footstool of Jehovah's feet for the heavens are His throne. Recognizing this, we are conscious that no earthly house built for Him is anything but a small matter. What is a great matter is the right spiritual state and attitude which should be found in man, who by nature is sinful and estranged from God. To be *poor* and *contrite* in spirit, and to receive the word as being truly the Word of God, and therefore to tremble at it and be governed by it — this invites the Divine regard. To such a man the Lord will look in blessing. We may remember that when the Lord Jesus opened His mouth on the mountain, the first beatitude He uttered was, "Blessed are the *poor* in spirit: for theirs is the kingdom of heaven" (Matthew 5:3).

But once more the prophet has to turn to the people, in their then existing state, with words of denunciation. They might be killing oxen, sacrificing lambs, offering oblation, burning incense, and yet all was an utter offence before God because their hearts were astray. They were anything but poor in spirit, but rather self-assertive, choosing their own ways and taking pleasure in abominable things. For this reason they came under God's judgment. Instead of calling upon God and receiving His immediate attention, He had called to them and they paid no attention whatever.

From these the prophet turned, in verse 5, once more to assure those who really did tremble at the word of God. They had been hated and cast out by the men of that day, and this they claimed to do in the name of the Lord and for His glory. We at once recognize that this is no uncommon thing. Something similar has happened again and again. It was thus when our Lord was on earth and in the days of the apostles. It has been so all too often in the sad history of Christendom, as witness the burning of "heretics" whether in Spain or in Britain. In Spain such an act was called by an expression which in English means "an act of *faith*", and since of faith of course, as they thought, to the glory of God.

The answer of the Lord to this kind of thing is not immediate but inevitable. The word is, "He shall appear to your joy, and they shall be ashamed." He SHALL — the thing is *determined* and *certain*, but it is *future*. The voice of the Lord will yet be heard, and when He speaks the thing is done. It will bring joy to the godly while a just recompence in judgment will be the portion of the enemies.

But now a further great prophetic fact comes before us. This mighty intervention of God, delivering His people and judging His foes, will be accompanied by a wonderful work of grace in the souls of those He will deliver. The earth will be made to bring forth in one day, and a nation will be born at once. The figure used in verse 7 indicates that this deliverance will be a "birth" which takes place in a way quite unexpected. So here we have Isaiah alluding to that great work of the Spirit of God, which is described more fully in Ezekiel 36:22-33, to which the Lord Jesus referred when He spoke to Nicodemus of being born "of water and of the Spirit".

Shall a nation be born at once? is the question asked in surprise. And the answer quite clearly is — Yes, it will. Of the old Israel, that the world has known, Moses had to complain at the start of their sad history, "They are a perverse and crooked generation...a very froward generation, children in whom is no faith" (Deuteronomy 32:5, 20). The Israel that will enter into millennial blessedness will be a new Israel, born again and therefore cleansed from their old life and ways. The Apostle Peter, writing to the scattered Jewish Christians of the early days, could say to them, "But ye are a chosen generation" (1 Peter 2:9), and he had previously spoken of their having been born again. As regards the new birth, converted Jews of today are advance samples of what will be wrought in the children of Israel, who finally enter the kingdom.

In view of this, all those who love Jerusalem, and at present mourn for her, may well rejoice. Her prosperity and glory will be a joy to behold. When the sons of Israel are a born-again nation, the saved of the nations will act toward them as a nursing mother, and peace will flow as a river, instead of there being resentment and disturbance on every side. The hand of God will be in all this, for His word is, "so will I comfort you".

But the prophet leaves us in no doubt as to what God's intervention will mean to the world at large. It will be the day when the inhabitants of the earth will learn righteousness, because God's judgments are in the earth, as Isaiah told us in chapter 26. Jehovah will come with fire and whirlwind and sword, as we see in verses 15 and 16, and when we turn to such a passage as Revelation 19, we discover that the Person who will thus come in judgment is no other than Jehovah-Jesus.

Verse 17 would indicate, we judge, that judgment will be specially severe against false religion — against those who practise abominable things, of an idolatrous nature, while professing to sanctify and purify themselves by them. Religious evil always incurs judgment of a very severe nature. This we see exemplified in our Lord's day. His strongest denunciations were directed against the Pharisees and Scribes.

The millennial reign will be preceded by the gathering together before God of the masses of mankind and before them the Divine glory will be displayed. The gathering of the nations that they may see the glory is described in verses 18 and 19, but the outcome of this is not described here. We turn to Matthew 25:31-46, and there we discover what will take place. All of them will be judged on the basis of their attitude towards the Son of Man, who is the King, as revealed by their treatment of messengers, who have represented Him, and whom He owns as His "brethren".

In Isaiah, however, the term used is "your brethren", for the prophet is more occupied with the regathering of the children of Israel from the most distant places to which they had been scattered. Their coming in this way will be like the bringing of an offering to God in a clean vessel — an offering therefore acceptable to Him and for His pleasure. Brought thus to the house of Jehovah, they will be taken for priests and Levites in the millennial age.

Now this was the original intention of God, as we see if we refer to Exodus 19:6. Had Israel kept the law that was delivered through Moses at Sinai, they would have been "a kingdom of priests". They broke the law, so this they never were. But the purpose of God is never defeated, and so here we are permitted to know that what failed then is ultimately achieved, as the fruit of the mercy of God. That it will be the fruit of MERCY is made very clear in the closing part of Romans 11.

Had it been brought about on a legal basis, some future breach of the law would imperil the whole position; as it stands on the basis of mercy, it is a permanent thing, as stable as the new heavens and new earth of the millennial age. From the overthrow of David's kingly line the world has seen a succession of kingdoms, rising up as the result of some overthrow, and each being overthrown in its turn, as predicted in Ezekiel 21:27; but here at last is a kingdom that abides.

And it will prove to be a kingdom in which Jehovah at last obtains His rightful place as the Object of worship. What He originally intended in connection with Israel, His people, will be fully accomplished, His glory will be in their midst; they will surround His house as a kingdom of priests; they will render Him due worship from one sabbath and new moon to another. He will have accomplished His original design.

The contemplation of these things is surely a great encouragement to us. We are not called to find our part in "My holy mountain Jerusalem", since our calling is a heavenly one, but we may rest assured that God will reach His original purpose with the church, as really and as fully as He will with Israel. Not one item of His good pleasure as to us will fail. And He will do it in such fashion as will command our glad recognition and worship. The saints in their heavenly seats will render a worship that will not need to be governed by sabbaths or new moons.

The last verse of our prophet is one of much solemnity. When Israel is regathered and blessed, and the earth rests in the blessedness indicated at the end of chapter 65, there will yet be a perpetual reminder of the awful result of rebellion and sin. When the Lord Jesus spoke of "the fire that never shall be quenched: where their worm dieth not" (Mark 9:43-44), it would seem that He alluded to this verse, and gave it an application stretching far beyond the millennial age. In "the lake of fire", which is "the second death" (Revelation 20:14), there will be an eternal witness to the awful effects of sin.

Let us rejoice in the greatness of the salvation that has reached us through our Lord Jesus Christ.

## OTHER BOOKS BY F. B. HOLE
## FROM SCRIPTURE TRUTH PUBLICATIONS

SALVATION

*ISBN 978-0-901860-17-0 (paperback)*
*211 pages; June 1998*

KEY TEACHINGS

*ISBN 978-0-901860-16-3 (paperback)*
*151 pages; June 1998*

"THE EPISTLE OF CHRIST" (EDITOR)

*ISBN 978-0-901860-73-6 (paperback)*
*140 pages; March 2008*

### *NEW TESTAMENT COMMENTARY SERIES:*

THE GOSPELS AND ACTS

*ISBN 978-0-901860-42-2 (paperback)*
*ISBN 978-0-901860-46-0 (hardback)*
*392 pages; February 2007*

ROMANS AND CORINTHIANS

*ISBN 978-0-901860-43-9 (paperback)*
*ISBN 978-0-901860-47-7 (hardback)*
*176 pages; February 2007*

GALATIANS TO PHILEMON

*ISBN 978-0-901860-44-6 (paperback)*
*ISBN 978-0-901860-48-4 (hardback)*
*204 pages; February 2007*

HEBREWS TO REVELATION

*ISBN 978-0-901860-45-3 (paperback)*
*ISBN 978-0-901860-49-1 (hardback)*
*304 pages; February 2007*

9 780901 860729